"Paul's book serves to prove that people can not only survive a stroke, but can be stroke *victors* instead of stroke *victims*."
—Rhonda Chatmon, Vice President, High Risk/Stroke Programs,
American Heart Association, Washington, DC

"I was inspired by Paul and his wife's relentless pursuit and attainment of a rich and productive life following a devastating stroke...I cannot think of anyone who would not profit enormously from this book...even those who haven't suffered disabilities or know people who have, will find this fascinating."
—Brenda Rapp, Ph.D., Cognitive Science Department
Johns Hopkins University

"This is to tell you how much I appreciated reading your autobiography, because although we are of a different generation, I'll be 69 next month, it is a true reflection of what a stroke victim has to go through...I wish you continued success in all your activities and accomplishments for both of us."
—Herbert Kaufman, stroke survivor, Antwerpen, Belgium

"Paul travels a compelling, inspiring and remarkable hero's journey through an unexpected life...It is an extremely powerful and motivating story. I didn't want to put the book down."
—Elaine R. Axelrod, Ph.D., Licensed Psychologist

"While there is no way someone can understand what it is like to suffer a stroke or other debilitating condition without actually experiencing it themselves, this book takes the reader about as close as you can come. I can't imagine anyone reading this without feeling your pain and frustration, or sharing in your triumphs...I think what sets this book apart...are the vivid pictures you have painted."
—Harry Weinstock, Executive Director,
Brain Injury Association of Virginia

"I, too, had a stroke at a young age...from reading your book I developed a focus...that I have not felt since the stroke."
—Peter Oyama, stroke survivor, Aiea, Hawaii

"There is a lesson to be learned here—of perseverance and unlimited hope. I make this book required reading for my students in speech pathology to inspire them never to give up."

—Darlene S. Williamson, MA, CCC-SLP, Adjunct Professor,
The George Washington University, Washington, DC

"I have been reading your book to my husband...he laughed and could certainly relate to all that you went through...you are a remarkable person and certainly a great inspiration for all of us. Thanks so much for sharing."

—Carol, spouse of a stroke survivor, Newport Beach, California

"I am about to graduate with a degree in the medical profession, and your story helped me to understand the experiences of my future patients. Because of your book, I will be more attentive to them as people and recognize that they can make enormous progress if they persevere."

—J.D.

"Your journey is a remarkable tale of victory over adversity after adversity after adversity. Paul and Stephanie make a great team and together you have conquered so much. By sharing your story you have provided hope and inspiration to so many."

—Peggy Cressy, RNC, MS, Director, Community Health
Operation Stroke, Inova Health System, Fairfax, Virginia

"You are an inspiration to anyone who has a disability...reading your book has given me a new slant on what I need to do. Thanks."

—Joyce Hoffman, Cohasset, Massachusetts

"This is a stirring story of how an energetic young couple in the prime of their lives manages when one of them is disabled by a catastrophic illness. I was frankly surprised by how readable and engaging the book is, as well as inspirational. The running narrative, with events unfolding in the style of a novel, kept me turning the pages. The dialogue and the attention to detail engage the reader's imagination."

—Harry Bacas, Former *Washington Star* newspaper
and *Nations Business* magazine writer

"Paul's commitment was an inspiration to people on Capitol Hill. His passion came through clearly, in spite of the extra challenges he faces."

—Charles E. Miller, Chairman and Founder, ProSpace-The Citizen's Space Lobby

"This book is a bright light for families experiencing a stroke or other life-changing event. So much of the information out there is clinical...here is a detailed, compassionate view of the struggles and rewards of dealing with a major life changing event. What's more, this book is a gripping page turner. I finished in it one evening and found myself yearning for more."

—Tracy Wahl, an Amazon.com reader, Washington, DC

"I just finished reading your super book! Paul, you're a great motivator for the disabled!"

—Robert Wilson, stroke survivor, New York, New York

"The courage you displayed in talking freely about your frustrations and triumphs is stunning, and I'm sure your victories will inspire many—including those who are fortunate enough to live without major disabilities."

—Keith Costa, Managing Editor, *Inside the Pentagon*, Arlington, VA

"Well done Paul. I suffered a left side paralyzing stroke 3 years ago, when I was just at the peak of a new profession...I understand your frustrations. People, especially the medical profession, are negative and give you little hope."

—John Morris, Australia

"All speech therapy has been stopped for my father, but after reading this book and seeing what 8 years of therapy has done for Paul, my family is looking into our options once again...People with aphasia are essentially trapped within their own body. Thanks, Paul for having the courage to move forward with your life and to tell your story. It truly gave me hope!!"

—An Amazon.com reader from South Lake Tahoe, California

"This book should be mandatory reading for anyone who is dealing with stroke and brain injured individuals."

—Lisa C. Koches, M.Ed., CCC-SLP, Fairfax, Virginia

"This is the second semester that I have used your book in my class. The students love it, and learn a great deal from your experience. I am sure that they will be better practitioners because of it."

—Doug Simmons, MS, OTR/L,
University of New Hampshire Occupational Therapy Department

"An excellent way for students to gain insight into the ways that a stroke alters everyday life."

—Becky M. Alwood, OT Student, UNH

"I just loved reading about the progression of Paul's recovery...It made something I've been learning about for 4 years real. It was eye opening...about what it really means to be client centered."

—Katherine Mertens, OT Student, UNH

"Talk about will power, Paul has the determination and courage of ten people times ten."

—Amy Wurster, OT Student, UNH

"It really showed me all the obstacles a stroke survivor must overcome in the home environment...This book truly is a testament to the struggle and dedication it takes to live life with a disability but also to love life with a passion."

—Sarah Gorham, OT Student, UNH

"Paul's life is evidence that great strides can continue to be made many years after a stroke."

—Deanna Desranleau, OT Student, UNH

"This book gives the reader the opportunity to experience a CVA the way Paul did, his strengths, weaknesses, losses and gains."

—Megan Connolly, OT Student, UNH

"An inspiring story, one that will change the way you think of your own life!"

—Courtney Marino, OT Student, UNH

"Paul's story provides hope to individuals who have a disability...as well as to those who are not disabled."

—Heather A. Hutchinson, OT Student, UNH

"The book did a fantastic job describing his emotions and experiences...Paul serves as a model of courage for everyone."

—Michael Harrington, OT Student, UNH

How to Conquer the World
With One Hand...And an Attitude

By
Paul E. Berger
and Stephanie Mensh

With Foreword By
Julian Whitaker, M.D.

Positive Power Publishing
Merrifield, Virginia

How to Conquer the World
With One Hand...And an Attitude

By Paul E. Berger
Winner of the 1999
Award for Individual Achievement
National Council on Communicative Disorders
and Stephanie Mensh

Second Edition
With Foreword By
Julian Whitaker, M.D.

Published by
Positive Power Publishing
P.O. Box 2644
Merrifield, Virginia 22116 U.S.A.
703-241-2375
Email: info@StrokeSurvivor.com
Visit our website at: www.StrokeSurvivor.com

ISBN 0-9668378-7-8

Library of Congress Catalog Card Number: 2002105068

Printed in Canada

Table of Contents

Acknowledgements

We wish to thank our parents, brothers, sisters, family and friends who gave us unconditional love and support throughout our lives and in the development of this book, without whom we could not have come so far, especially Joe Mensh and Edie Berger, who we miss dearly. Special thanks to the doctors, and dedicated therapists and tutors who spent years providing speech, physical and occupational therapy. And thank you to the teachers, tutors, counselors and employers who have made it possible to change careers and find fulfilling work.

We also wish to thank Curtis Colby for helping us to get started on this book; Peggy Dace, for her support and special connections; Ellen Klein for editorial assistance; Nina Tisara of Tisara Photography, Inc. for photography; and Marida Hines of Dog Days Graphics, for cover and text design.

Foreword

by Julian Whitaker, M.D.

As my patients and the readers of my books and newsletter, *Health & Healing*, know, I have dedicated my medical career to helping people achieve optimal health through nutrition, exercise, and lifestyle changes.

I have found myself continually challenging the conventional thinking of the medical establishment, which often views surgery or potent prescription drugs as the only way to treat patients. And unlike many of my medical colleagues—I learn a lot from my patients.

I believe that an ounce of prevention is worth a pound of cure. I know it is possible to reverse the effects of heart disease, high blood pressure, and diabetes, and so lower the risk of heart attack and stroke. It is always better *not* to have the heart attack or stroke. But if you have suffered and survived a stroke, there is plenty that you can do to recover and live life to its fullest.

One of the most inspiring and uplifting stories of stroke recovery I've seen is Paul Berger's. Paul and his wife Stephanie Mensh, a former editor of *Health & Healing*, faced many obstacles following Paul's stroke at the young age of 36. They challenged the conventional thinking of medical and rehabilitation professionals. It took guts, and a never-give-up attitude.

Paul's spirit and willingness to take "the road less traveled" to reach his goals reminds me in some ways of my own journey through conventional and alternative medicine. Like Paul, I was driven by what I knew was right. Paul believed in himself, forged his own path, and his "impossible" achievements eventually proved others wrong.

How to Conquer the World With One Hand...And an Attitude is a road map for stroke survivors and others who have endured major life changes—and for their families and the professionals who work with them. Yet it is also an amazing, life-affirming story for all to enjoy and learn from.

Julian Whitaker, M.D.

Introduction
by Paul E. Berger

This book is about how I overcame a life-changing crisis, coped with the challenge of redefining myself, then went on to turn my dreams into achievable goals. This is about having an attitude to fight and win, and having fun along the way.

Many inspirational books just take you through the person's crisis period. I wanted to show how much you can achieve afterwards. I had a devastating stroke at age 36. One year later, I was able to return to "normal," at least from an outsider's point-of-view. But I discovered that I didn't and couldn't return to the way I was before the stroke. Routine activities became new challenges—daily disappointments to swallow and small victories to savor.

My story spans more than 10 years. I tested myself, gritted my teeth through embarrassing moments, and fought off depression and anger. I never gave up, or accepted my disabilities. Instead, I focused on my strengths and redirected my goals. I fueled my attitude with the positive support from family and friends, and ignored the people who said it couldn't be done. I proved that with stubborn determination, I could set my sights on a new world and conquer it. And I won.

A special note to people who have suffered a stroke or other major setback: Don't give up. Don't let others tell you to retire, go away, or hide from life. I want my story to inspire you and your family, friends and professionals to help you live your life as you want to. Stay active, go back to work, back to your favorite hobbies and sports, and volunteer to help others.

If you have a second chance at life, as I did, don't waste it feeling sorry for yourself or worrying about what's wrong with you. Focus on the good things and reach for your dreams.

Who would think that a stroke survivor with a severe language disability could write a book? My answer is this book. I did it—*with one hand...and an attitude.* Although I got some writing help from my wife, this is my story. I hope you'll enjoy it as much as I have.

Prologue

I was 36 and had everything I wanted: a rewarding career, a happy marriage and a promising future. My investments were doing well, and I'd just bought a new car. I owned a house and was saving for a bigger one. I was in control of my life and, if I took a rare moment to think about it, I felt like a conqueror.

I was a type-A personality, which I knew could be bad for my health. My father already had suffered two heart attacks, and I didn't want to follow in his footsteps. So I watched my weight, was careful about what I ate and worked out at the gym three or four times a week. I was in great shape and felt energetic and powerful.

My story begins on December 30, 1985. In just two days, it would be the New Year, and I was eagerly anticipating a major change in my career.

At that time, I was working for the Washington, D.C., city government. I had a master's degree in Urban Affairs and Policy Analysis and had a position in the city's real estate development department. My job was to facilitate the construction of downtown projects, making it easier for buildings to get built and open their doors to the public. I had chosen to work for the government because I wanted to help build a better world. I liked driving around town and seeing the results of my work. Lately, however, I had become frustrated with the city bureaucracy and had decided to look for a new job.

By going to school at night, I had recently earned an MBA in Finance from a college in Arlington, Virginia, where my wife, Stephanie, and I lived. With this added credential, I was looking at jobs in either finance or real estate. I'd had several promising interviews and had just been asked by one company to return for a follow-up meeting after New Year's.

So, on December 30th, when Stephanie dropped me off at the gym and went shopping for a dress to wear on New Year's Eve, I knew my life was about to change. What I didn't know was that it would change as dramatically as it did....

3

Part 1:
Surviving the Crisis

The Explosion in My Head
December 30, 1985-January 1986

I'd finished jogging around the track and <u>had just started</u> <u>lifting weights when, all of a sudden, I got a terrible headache.</u> I went over to the gym attendant and asked for an aspirin.

"Sorry," she said. "We're not allowed to give out anything, not even aspirin. What's wrong?"

"I have the worst headache." The pain already was so bad that I was starting to see double.

"I can call an ambulance for you," she offered, "but that's all I can do."

Why not call an ambulance? I thought. *If it turns out to be nothing, I'll be a little embarrassed; but this feels really bad, and I should check it out.* "Okay," I decided, "call an ambulance."

I started toward the locker room to change out of my jogging shorts. But pain and dizziness overwhelmed me, and I barely staggered to a table and chair a few feet away. I landed in the chair, then lay my head on the table. I don't know how long I sat slumped like that; my sense of time was becoming distorted.

"Sir, how are you?" the paramedic asked.

"I don't feel so good." I told him about my headache.

"Okay, let me help you onto the gurney."

"Can you take me to —— Hospital?" I wanted to go there because it was affiliated with my HMO and had a very good reputation. But it was located across the Potomac River, in Washington, D.C.

"No. We have to take you to the nearest hospital." This turned out to be a small, community hospital.

Later I wondered if my story might have unfolded differently, had I been taken directly to the hospital I'd requested.

The paramedic wrapped a blanket around me and wheeled

me out. It seemed like miles before we reached the ambulance and even longer before we arrived at the hospital. By the time I got to the emergency room, I thought my head was going to explode.

Suddenly I remembered that Stephanie would be on her way to the gym to pick me up. The paramedic called the gym and found her already there.

"Hello, Mrs. Berger? I'm here with Paul, in the emergency room. He wants you to go into his locker and bring his clothes, wallet and coat. He left everything behind when we brought him here."

Then he turned to me and said, "She wants to know the combination to your lock."

I rattled off the numbers, and he repeated them into the phone.

"She says she'll be here in a few minutes."

The emergency room was quiet that evening. I lay on a bed in a dark, curtained-off area, waiting for Stephanie to arrive with my things. The pain in my skull was so intense that I had no idea how much time had passed before she finally appeared. She told me it was ten p.m. and explained that I'd given her the wrong combination to my locker. The staff at the gym had to break the lock so she could get my things.

At that point, the neurosurgeon on call showed up.

"Can you describe what happened?" he asked.

Gritting my teeth from the pain, I told him everything I remembered.

"Do you suffer from migraines?"

"No."

"Are you having double vision?"

"Yes."

The neurosurgeon raised an eyebrow.

"Do you know what day it is?"

I think I answered correctly.

"I'm going to order a CT scan," he said. "Someone will be down in a few minutes to take you there, Mr. Berger."

By the time the CT scan results were available, it was near midnight. The neurosurgeon admitted me to the intensive care unit and ordered painkillers and other medication.

He told me that a blood vessel in my brain had ruptured, and blood was flooding my brain, causing the pain. He said that this was very serious; in fifty percent of the cases, the person dies. He said that I was lucky I had come to the hospital right away, and that he thought I would be okay.

He asked me how old I was. Stephanie answered, "Thirty-six."

"Me, too," he said. "But for the grace of God, this could be me," he told us. "This can happen to anyone, at any age."

Luckily for us, Stephanie worked for a national association representing surgeons. The next morning, before returning to the hospital, she called her boss, Matty, to ask for her help. Matty had many high-level connections within the medical community. Stephanie asked her to check the neurosurgeon's credentials and find out more about my diagnosis, a "subarach-noid ruptured aneurysm on the carotid artery."

When Stephanie arrived at the hospital, I was still in a great deal of pain. My area of the ICU was darkened. Bright lights, loud noises or other intense stimulation could cause further bleeding, the neurosurgeon had said.

"How do you feel?" Stephanie asked.

"Okay," I answered automatically. "No. Not okay. My head still hurts."

I stared into the dark room for a few minutes. Stephanie said nothing, trying to take in all of the monitoring equipment hooked up to me. I breathed heavily, to fight back the pain.

"You have to get my health insurance card. You have my wallet. And call them. It's an HMO. You have to call them and tell them I'm here. They have to know for the insurance cover-age."

Then the neurosurgeon came into the room.

"I have some papers for you to sign. You must have an angiogram so we can locate the aneurysm. When we locate it, we will be able to operate right away. It is a radiological test. We inject dye into your leg, then trace the blood flow with x-rays through the vessels up in the neck and head.

"I'll probably transfer you to a university hospital for the surgery. They will know better how to care for you there for this situation. The literature shows that operating within seventy-two hours for patients like you, Mr. Berger, have the very best outcome."

He gave me a clipboard with the informed consent release papers for the test.

The very best outcome...Seventy-two hours... The words echoed in my mind. I was sure I would have the best outcome; I always did well on tests. I figured everything would be back to normal in a few days, and I'd forget the whole incident like a bad dream.

About an hour later, I was taken to the radiology department for the angiogram, and Stephanie headed for the telephone. She called Matty, who reported that the neurosurgeon was good. But she added that everyone had told her I should be moved immediately to a university hospital. She gave Stephanie the names of the top neurosurgeons at the university hospitals in the Washington, D.C., area, including the one that was partnered with my HMO. Stephanie had already called my primary care physician, Dr. Lanman, and this was where he was having me transferred.

Matty also said that the experts advised that the angiogram be performed by a radiologist who specialized in neurologic imaging. I was undergoing the test with a general radiologist. Not a good omen.

Stephanie then called the neurosurgeon recommended by Matty's contacts, Dr. King, at the hospital to which I was being transferred. She asked him to take my case, and he readily agreed.

8

Next, she canceled our New Year's Eve plans. Our friends Jerry and Marie were supposed to come down from my hometown of Philadelphia to be with us. We'd also had tickets to fly to St. Martin the next weekend; perhaps Jerry and Marie would go on our trip instead.

Finally, Stephanie called my office and tried to explain what was happening. She said that the call wasn't easy for her. We had many more questions than answers to convey at that point.

Stephanie and I spent New Year's Eve in the ICU. The staff was kind enough to let her stay as long as she wished.

When I was single and didn't have a date or a party on New Year's Eve, I felt like the world was going to end. This time, although I had my wife at my side, <u>my world as I knew it had ended</u>.

The next morning, after Stephanie had returned to the hospital, the neurosurgeon came by on his rounds.

"I examined the angiogram," he said sadly. "I know exactly where the aneurysm should be, but I cannot find it on the film. It is possible that the bleeding is obscuring the aneurysm," he huffed.

"If I could see where it was, I would operate immediately. In Europe, they would let me operate and find the aneurysm during surgery. But in the United States, they do not allow it; the threat of malpractice. Even though I know where it should be, and you should have this surgery as soon as possible."

This was a terrible blow. Matty's warning that a specialist should perform the angiogram echoed loudly in my mind.

"Is it the quality of the angiogram? It wasn't done well by the general radiologist, was it?" Stephanie asked, trying to stay calm.

"I don't know," he replied. "There is too much blood to see where an aneurysm might be."

"I've talked to Paul's HMO," Stephanie said. "They're

9

transferring him to the university hospital this morning."

"That's okay," he said graciously. "I will be happy to provide them consultation on Mr. Berger's case."

When the ambulance driver came, Stephanie told him no sirens; a slow, quiet, easy ride. She would follow in her car. My head still hurt, and I was glad to be leaving. I was sure that Dr. Lanman and Dr. King would get moving on my case, solve the pain, and get me back on my feet.

Soon after I was admitted to the university hospital's neurosurgery floor, Dr. Lanman came to see me. He became our go-between with the other health care professionals and served as our "translator." He explained all the neurosurgery terms and described what we should expect. He was my age, energetic and concerned for me. I often have thought that I received a little extra effort because I was the same age as most of the doctors and nurses. Were they also thinking that "there but for the grace of God go I?"

For the next few days, I stayed in bed. The hospital room was dark, and I wasn't allowed a TV. The doctors wanted to limit any stimulation that might cause additional bleeding in my brain. I had no appetite, had trouble urinating and continued to suffer a constant, throbbing pain in my skull, despite the medication and isolation. I could still read, write and talk, but most of the time I said little.

Day and night, Stephanie sat near me in the dark room, watching me; watching my blood pressure monitor registering near 200 over 150 (normal is 120 over 80), my heartbeat slightly arrhythmic. I could see that she was overwhelmed with concern. But neither of us realized how close to death I was. We were just too young to understand the meaning of death—or life.

"Paul, I have to call your parents. What should I say?" Stephanie asked later that week.

"Tell them I'm okay. Tell them not to come. They should enjoy their vacation in Florida. It's too cold and icy here.

Besides, it might be too much stress for Dad."

Stephanie called. "I want to talk to him," my mother insisted.

"They're not allowing a phone in his room just yet," Stephanie said, not telling my mother that the loud ringing could trigger more bleeding.

"Stephanie, anytime anything is involved with the brain, it is really serious," Mom said. "Should we come to Washington?"

"No. Let's see how these tests go for the next few days. Paul just doesn't feel he's sick enough."

Stephanie promised to call every day with an update on my progress. But mothers always have ways to find out about their children. That evening, when Stephanie returned home, the phone was ringing. It was Jonathan, my high school friend, a doctor. His parents are good friends of my parents. My mother had called him in Philadelphia and urged him to contact Stephanie.

Stephanie repeated all the medical terms, tests and information she had gathered in the past few days. "They just can't seem to find the aneurysm. And Dr. King now isn't even sure it is an aneurysm. He said he can't see anything on the angiogram; there's too much blood. Please don't say anything about this to Paul's parents. We don't want them to worry."

"Well, if it is an aneurysm," Jonathan said, "the conventional wisdom is that whatever functions the person has right after the bleeding is where he'll be, or less. For example, if Paul could not talk or write now," he said, "there would be little hope that he would regain that after the surgery to close the aneurysm. Did they say anything about that?"

"I don't think so, and Paul is talking and reading and writing. He can still walk, although they aren't letting him out of bed."

"Well, that sounds positive. Call me if you need anything."

The next day, Dr. Lanman told us about some new equipment that had been delivered to my room. The bleeding in my brain had caused swelling and pressure. Sometimes, to alleviate the pressure, the neurosurgeons drill little holes in the skull. The equipment was there if they needed to do so.

This was a blow.

"I thought Paul was getting better," Stephanie said weakly.

"Well, let's hope they don't need to use it," he said, trying to be comforting.

Stephanie made some notes in a little pocket notebook. There was so much information and new terminology that keeping notes had become her only way to cope. Every few hours, in my dark room, she squinted to write down my blood pressure readings, medications and comments from the nurses or doctors. She had started to collect important phone numbers, too, including Dr. Lanman's direct line, which she later used more than once.

Finally, a full week had passed since my headache had started. The pain had dulled somewhat, either from the medication, reduced swelling or just having lived with it for so long.

Dr. King ordered a second angiogram. He explained that, because my condition appeared to have stabilized, enough blood should have cleared to see where the bleeding had originated and to make a decision on the next step in treatment.

This time, the test was performed by a neuroradiologist, a specialist in interpreting images of the brain. After a few minutes, he located the aneurysm. He grumbled, then said, "Dr. King will take a look at this and discuss your options." I didn't want to know any more.

When I returned to my room, Stephanie was waiting. I told her what the neuroradiologist had said, but I didn't feel like talking about it. I knew that Stephanie wanted me to have surgery. She wanted the doctors to perform their medical miracles and make me completely well again. I didn't feel the same way. I didn't want surgery; I didn't feel that sick. And deep inside, I was too scared to breathe.

I knew things were bad when Dr. King sat down at my bedside to talk to me about the angiogram. "Now that we know where it is, I can see the aneurysm on the first film," he said. "We have to operate."

"What other choices do I have?"

"If we don't operate, you could die from the bleeding."

"Can I die from the surgery?"

"You can die from the roof of the grocery store falling on your head. In this institution, under my care, no one dies from this operation."

"I just don't know."

"How soon would you schedule the operation?" Stephanie asked. "His family wants to come in to be with us for this."

"Well...today's Thursday.... Paul is stable, getting a little better.... We could schedule it for Monday." Then he stressed, "Paul, you have to have this surgery."

"Tell me a little more about what you do," I said, trying to concentrate. My mind was a blur, grogged out from the medication and now this heart-stopping news.

"This is not a difficult operation. It's our bread-and-butter procedure," he explained, trying to soften his clipped manner. "An aneurysm is a bump on your carotid artery. Yours is about the size of a large marble, and it's well-defined. It's something you've probably had since birth, and it could have burst at any time; last week, or fifty years from now picking up a bag of groceries, or any sudden physical exertion, like lifting weights. We open the skull, reach down and put a platinum fastener over the aneurysm. If nothing goes wrong, you should be able to leave the hospital in a week or so, then recover at home for about a month or two."

"What do you think?" I asked Stephanie, stalling for time, trying to clear my thoughts so I could reason this out.

"I think you should have the surgery. I don't see that there is any choice. If Dr. King doesn't operate, the aneurysm can continue to bleed and...."

"Okay." I felt beaten down and frustrated by this total loss of control over my life. This feeling would soon become an unwelcome constant.

According to Stephanie's notes, Dr. King also told her I could have a stroke, become paralyzed, lose my speech, not work again. But she didn't really hear or believe him. She simply assumed I would do well and that our lives soon would return to normal.

Stephanie didn't get back to the hospital until late the following day. I missed her. I was bored in the dark, with no TV, no light to read by, no concentration to think.

After going to her office to thank Matty for her support, Stephanie had gone to a medical library to read everything she could find and understand about aneurysms, making copious entries in her pocket notebook and adding to her list of questions for the doctors. Among other things, she learned that the platinum clip implanted in my brain to seal the aneurysm wouldn't set off a metal detector or be disturbed by cabin pressure on an airplane. This was good news, because we traveled to Europe at least once a year, and she was sure we'd be traveling again in the near future.

Meanwhile, my blood pressure continued to rise. To lower it, I was transferred to the ICU for intravenous medication.

As news of my impending surgery spread, I was visited by a parade of family, friends and coworkers. Even the head of my department, about five levels above me in the bureaucratic hierarchy, came to see me. This was so unexpected that I got scared.

"Why are they doing this? Am I really this sick?" I was angry and confused. Stephanie didn't know what to say.

My parents flew in from Florida, and my brother, Stanley, caught a flight from San Francisco, where he was living. They planned to stay just a few days, based on Stephanie's upbeat assessment of my condition. They eventually stayed nearly two weeks, waiting until they were sure I would survive.

I didn't like being the object of all this attention. I was tormented by the unrelenting pain in my head, fearful of the upcoming surgery and frustrated by not being allowed out of bed. I reacted by being defiant. Late that night, on the eve of my surgery, I begged my nurse to help me get out of bed.

I wanted to sit on the commode, I said. Once in the bathroom, I sat there, trying to remember what to do. Suddenly, my head exploded again.

I tried to call for the nurse, but I don't know if any words came out. I don't know how much time passed, only that I was back in hell.

The next thing I knew, I was undergoing another CT scan. My aneurysm had opened again, flooding my brain with a fresh tide of blood.

As I was being wheeled back to the ICU, I saw Stephanie and Stanley. It was morning, and they had come to wish me good luck. Despite the sudden, new bleeding, Dr. King had decided to operate.

My last words to them, pushed out through unbearable pain, were: "Let's get this over with!" Looking back, I wish I'd said something more memorable, because it would be a very long time before I would speak again.

Lost in Space
January 1986

My brain surgery was supposed to take about three hours. My family was in the waiting room, anxiously watching the time. But there was no sign of Dr. King. Things obviously were not going well.

Finally, after nearly six hours, Dr. King burst into the waiting room, still in his green surgical scrubs and cap. "Last night, I left a much different patient than I faced this morning. The nurse let him out of bed against my orders, and Paul had a second bleed. We were working on an *angry red brain*. To operate or not operate: We went in to save what we could. The next twenty-four hours are critical. Then the next few days will tell if he'll pull through."

Dr. King searched for something optimistic to say. "I was able to get a response from Paul in the recovery room, but he's very withdrawn."

I awoke in the recovery room, a large, open area similar to the ICU. My headache was gone; I felt mellow and sleepy. When I opened my eyes, it was like looking through the wrong end of a pair of binoculars. The world seemed blurry and far away.

I heard a nurse call my name. Then she touched my face. "I'm going to open your eyes and shine a light in." Just as I heard the end of her sentence, I was blinded by a bright light. I tried to close my eyes, but the nurse's fingers held my lids apart. Later, Stephanie explained that the nurse was checking my reflexes. She wanted to see how my pupils dilated; a routine I endured countless times as the days went on.

"Hi, Paul," Stephanie said. I could sense her standing near me, but she sounded far away. She asked me something, but I couldn't catch the meaning. I tried to speak, but nothing came out.

Stephanie lifted my hand and placed it on my face. I didn't

know I had on an oxygen mask. Or that my head was bandaged. I had a tube draining fluid from my head, and there was a tube in each arm. I tried to open my eyes to look at her, but I was too tired.

For the rest of the day, Stephanie, my mother, father and brother took turns visiting me. I felt like I was dreaming, and every now and then a face would peek at me through the clouds. Sometimes I opened my eyes and tried to smile or nod, to let them know I appreciated their being there.

Then I heard another voice. "Paul, how are you?"

I opened my eyes. It was Dr. King. I nodded, trying to thank him for making the pain go away and tell him I was okay.

"Good, good," he said. "Paul, you're doing fine. Keep it up."

I couldn't understand what he was saying, but he seemed pleased. *I must be doing okay,* I thought. I wanted to respond, but all I could do was make a thumbs-up sign.

My family stopped visiting; they must have gone home for the night. I lost track of time, drifting in and out of sleep; being prodded awake by nurses and startled by bright lights.

I didn't know that my life was hanging in the balance, that my body was waging a desperate battle. I didn't know how much my family was worrying about me. Maybe it was better that I didn't know.

The next morning, Stephanie and my brother arrived in time to see a technician wheeling me out of the ICU to get another CT scan. Stephanie told me later that she thought the side of my face looked droopy, and she was sure I'd suffered a stroke.

When I returned from the CT scan, my family was allowed to see me. Stephanie and my mother came in first. "Does it hurt? Are you in pain, Sweetie?" Mom asked, stroking my cheek.

I wasn't sure what she was saying, but it was soothing to hear her voice and feel her hand, so I nodded.

About an hour later, Dr. King broke the news to my family: "Paul has had a *massive* stroke." Although Stephanie had guessed it, she felt stunned and defeated to hear the doctor confirm it. "It could have been a result of the rebleeding Sunday night; or of the vasospasms, the uncontrollable constrictions of the sensitive blood vessels in the brain, caused by the pressure of the bleeding; or unknown reasons," he said.

"What does it mean?" my mother asked.

"Well, through therapy, Paul may be able to say a few words," he replied, trying to give them some hope. "The CT scan shows that a very large area of the left side of the brain has been affected. Was Paul left handed?"

Stephanie shook her head, "No."

"For some left-handed patients, the speech centers are on the opposite side of the brain," he explained. "I was hoping that perhaps Paul's dominant side wasn't hit."

He paused and searched for something encouraging to say. "Well, according to the CT scan, Paul should be unconscious. But he's not. He just gave me a thumbs-up when I asked him how he felt. That's a good sign. Let's see how he does over the next few days."

The effects of my surgery began to show. My eyes swelled nearly shut. They were black and blue, as if I'd been savagely mugged.

"Mr. Berger, I'm going to look in your eyes," the ICU nurse said. This time it really hurt as she pried my lids apart. The light hurt too.

"Push against my hand," she said. My left hand had a little strength to push, but I couldn't get my right hand to do anything. The nurse pushed my feet. I could respond with my left foot; but the right, nothing.

Later, Dr. King did the same, with an entourage of residents looking on. Suddenly I heard Stephanie gasp; Dr. King had just stuck his pen under my right toenail. I didn't feel a thing.

"How do you feel, Paul?" he asked. I wanted to say I was

okay. The oxygen mask had been replaced by a small tube in my nose, but I still couldn't make a sound.

At the last minute, I remembered to give him a thumbs-up sign. That effort alone, exhausted me. I didn't fight the sleep.

Mid-week, Dr. King removed my bandages. I didn't actually see myself until much later, but Stephanie told me how I looked. A little stubble was starting to grow on the shaved half of my head, and there was a six-inch scar, like a zipper, curving from the top of my head down to my ear. My face was swollen; my eyes bruised shut. "You look like Frankenstein's monster," she joked.

Dr. Lanman stopped by to see me. "Paul, how are you?" he asked. I shook my head. He didn't know what I meant, but he tried to be reassuring.

"I've been talking to your family. It's good to see them here. Family support is so important during this crucial time," he said.

The following day, Dr. King gave my family more bad news. "Paul's lung has collapsed. He has aspirational pneumonia. It's caused by fluids collecting in the lungs when the patient can't clear his throat. Paul's muscles on his right side are paralyzed from the stroke, including the muscles used in swallowing. This is a common complication of strokes."

"Can he die from the pneumonia?" Stephanie asked.

"Paul's not in the clear, yet," he said. "But, if he makes it through the weekend, he'll be on his way. Paul is young and strong and has a good chance. His CT scan showed such a massive stroke, he should be in a coma, but he's not. That's a good sign. I think he'll pull through this."

"If he can't swallow, how will he eat?" my mother asked.

"There's a tube going into his stomach with liquid food. And therapists have techniques to overcome the swallowing problems."

Dr. King left to continue his rounds.

A friend of ours who is a speech pathologist came to visit me in the ICU. Becki told Stephanie to urge the doctor to start me on speech, physical and occupational therapy immediately. She said that the sooner therapy starts, the better for the patient.

Stephanie asked Dr. Lanman to write an order for therapy, and he did. The following day, three young women examined me in the ICU. They looked dour. I was so weak from the surgery and complications, and still had a fever from the pneumonia. They said that it was too early to start therapy, but they had their orders.

I knew that they'd make me better again, and I tried to cooperate. For the most part, that meant keeping my eyes open and my mind focused on what they were doing and saying. They moved my arms and legs. They talked to me, although I didn't always understand their questions. And they made notes.

By the weekend, I was feeling a little better. I could breathe easier and stay awake for longer periods. My chest and eyes felt less painful. The terrible headache I'd had for the two weeks before the surgery hadn't come back. I was sure that, once I'd built up my strength, I'd be up and around. Clearly, I didn't know yet what it meant to have had a stroke.

Finally, a week after the surgery, I was moved into a private room. The nurses propped me up with pillows almost into a sitting position. It felt good to be able to look around, feel more in control. The fog was starting to lift. I could see walls, doors, and the window. I could tell when it was daytime. I was more aware of people coming and going, and I could focus better on their questions.

Best of all, my family could visit with me as long as they wished. I hadn't known they'd been limited to ten-minute visits each hour when I was in the ICU. I was happy to have their company. It made me feel that I was making progress. This positive feeling was reinforced when my parents and brother decided it was okay for them to go home.

Stephanie seemed more upbeat when she came in that afternoon. She showed me get-well cards from my friends and coworkers. I looked at one closely; turned it around, upside down, but it didn't make any sense to me. At first I thought it was a joke card; then I decided that the medication I was taking must be clouding my thinking. I tried to tell her this, but the words wouldn't come. So I pointed to the card, gesturing in circles to say it looked mixed up to me. She nodded her understanding and read the card out loud. I listened to her voice, trying to make sense of the words. I knew the message meant that people cared about me and were cheering for my quick recovery. But the words, the names, were blurs.

I tried to tell Stephanie how much I appreciated the cards. "I know you're trying to tell me something," she said. "Do you want a pen and paper? I'll get them for you."

She ran out of the room and came back a few minutes later with a clipboard. She put a pencil in my left hand. I was right-handed, so the pencil felt awkward. I looked at it, trying to remember what to do with it. I couldn't remember which end to use, and turned it over a few times, trying to figure it out. Stephanie gently positioned it in my hand, with the tip touching the paper.

I tried to write, "Thank you for the cards." I felt the pencil move across the paper.

"I don't understand," Stephanie said, looking over my shoulder. I looked down at the page. I'd made a black squiggle that I couldn't read, either. This was more than I could deal with. I was frustrated and too tired to keep trying, so I pushed the clipboard away and closed my eyes. *My body just needs more time and rest,* I thought.

"I'll come back a little later," Stephanie said, taking the clipboard and get-well cards with her.

When Stephanie came in the next morning, I realized how much I'd missed her. I tried to say hello, but nothing came out.

She smiled, and said, "You look better." She told me about my many friends in Philadelphia who'd heard through the grapevine about my stroke and had called her to ask about my progress. I had trouble concentrating on what she was saying.

After letting her ramble on for a few minutes, I tried to

21

change the topic of the conversation. I'd thought of something I wanted to tell her. Nothing came out, so I tried gesturing to her, holding up my left hand.

"Is something wrong?" she asked, realizing that I was trying to communicate.

I shook my head, then nodded. Nothing was wrong. I held up my hand again, this time turning it back and forth.

"Stop? Are you telling me you want me to stop something? To have the doctors or nurses stop something?" she guessed, trying to comprehend this new gesture.

Again, I shook my head. I moved my hand closer to Stephanie, so she could see my fingers.

"Are you pointing to something?" she guessed again, looking around the room.

This was frustrating. I didn't know how to communicate with her. She just wasn't getting it. I shook my head and my hand.

I knew I had to get through to her, so I pulled myself together. I turned my hand around, looking at it, hoping she would see what I was looking at.

"I don't know what you want," Stephanie said, trying not to sound discouraged. "Would the nurse know what you mean?"

Again, I shook my head and motioned with my hand. *Come on, you have to know this,* I thought, not understanding why she couldn't get it.

"Is there something wrong with your hand?" she asked. "Does it hurt?"

YES! YES! It's my hand! I thought, shaking my head.

"It's not your hand?" Stephanie said, seeing me shake my head. I didn't know that because of the stroke, I was shaking my head "no" when I meant to nod "yes."

I tried to be patient, since she almost had figured it out. I motioned with my hand again, but before she could venture another guess, the nurse came in to do her routine checks. After

22

the nurse left, our guessing game resumed and went on throughout most of the day.

"Is it about your hand?" Stephanie asked for the tenth time. "Your nails? Your fingernails?"

Finally! I smiled and pointed my finger at her triumphantly.

"Your fingernails!" she laughed, very excited that she had guessed it at last. She ran out of the room to find a nurse.

"I'm sorry, we can't cut a patient's nails," the nurse told her, mentioning something about liability for diabetic infections.

"Can I do it?" Stephanie asked, unwilling to let the system ignore my needs.

"Yes, I'll get you some scissors," the nurse said.

The scissors were too dull to clip my fingernails. "Don't worry, I'll bring clippers from home," Stephanie reassured me. "I just can't believe that with all the terrible things you're going through now, all you can think about is cutting your nails!"

The next day, I was moved to a double room; a sign of my continuing improvement. I didn't like having to share a room and was a little confused about what was going on.

Dr. Lanman came to see me and explained that the room I'd been in, right by the nurses station, was reserved for the worst cases, so the nurses could watch the patients more closely. Now that I was getting better, I could be moved down the hall.

My roommate was a middle-aged man with a back problem. He asked me a few questions, trying to make conversation. I tried to answer, but nothing came out.

When my speech therapist came in, she explained to me and my roommate that I'd suffered a stroke. *Stroke?! I thought only old people had strokes. How could I, a healthy, athletic, thirty-six-year-old, have had a stroke?* I was overwhelmed by the news. But at least I finally understood why nothing came out when I tried to talk.

Some time later, a nurse and attendant lifted me out of bed into a chair for the first time since my surgery. I was happy to be getting out of bed, but scared by the sensation of being lifted and having no control over my body. I struggled to make my arms and legs obey me, but they wouldn't. I couldn't even hold myself upright in the chair and almost fell out. The attendant grabbed me while the nurse took a spare sheet and tied it around my waist and the chair to hold me in.

"Here's your call button and the channel-changer for the TV, Paul," the nurse said, placing the equipment on the arm of the chair near my left hand and patting it. "I'll be back in a little while to check on you."

I suddenly had a flashback to the previous year, when I'd been carried down a ski slope on a stretcher. I'd collided with a tree, not being able to make a sharp turn on the steep trail, which had iced over that morning. After the concussion, I rested for a day and then was back on the slopes. *Why am I taking so long to recover now?* I wondered, beginning to sense the wrongness of my situation.

I slowly took inventory of my body. There were plastic inflators wrapped around my legs. Dr. Lanman later explained that these were to prevent blood clots and keep the blood circulating until I could walk again. There were tubes in my arms and an irritating tube in my nose that snaked down my throat into my stomach. I reached up and touched it. *What is this?* Reflexively, I pulled it out; then started to gag.

"Paul, hey! What are you doing!" my roommate shouted. "Nurse, nurse! We need help in here!" he yelled.

A nurse came running in. "Paul, Paul, what have you done!"

I don't know. It bothered me. What's wrong? I thought, as her reaction began to alarm me. I started to shake a little and felt very woozy.

"What a mess!" she exclaimed, as she dabbed at the brown, sticky fluid dripping out of the feeding tube onto my hospital gown and "sheet-belt." She bundled up the tube and said, "Stay

24

in the chair for a few more minutes, Paul, while I get someone to help me. And I'll call to get this put back in."

Later that day, Stephanie came in to visit. She had started a routine of visiting briefly on her way to her office, working for a few hours, then returning to the hospital for the afternoon and evening, not leaving until well after visiting hours were over.

"The nurse said you sat up in a chair today. That's great!" she said.

Her positive attitude sounded good. I smiled and nodded.

"She said you sat up for almost an hour."

Yes, I remember being in the chair, I thought. I nodded again.

Stephanie was stroking my left hand. Her touch felt nice.

"The nurse said you pulled out your feeding tube," she ventured. "Did you do that, or did the nurse?" She wasn't convinced that I had pulled out the tube, even though I didn't really know what I was doing. She was inclined to believe that the hospital staff made mistakes and then tried to cover them up by blaming me. She touched the tube in my nose.

I remembered the technician taking me to another room to have the tube put back in. *I don't want it,* I thought.

"You pulled it out?" Stephanie said, almost reading my thoughts. "You need this tube. It's feeding you. Do you understand? You need the food to build up your strength. You can't swallow yet. That's why you had pneumonia. They're afraid that if you try to eat or drink, you'll inhale food into your lungs. It will make you very sick."

I could tell she was angry and tried to concentrate on what she was saying. But I thought, *I'm angry, too. I want to eat real food!* I gestured to my mouth, showing that I wanted to feed myself.

Stephanie saw the stubborn determination in my face. "You want to eat?" She was getting better at understanding my gestures.

"I'll ask Dr. Lanman to order a swallowing test soon. They

25

have to test you before they'll let you try to eat."

I nodded. *That's fine.*

On her way out, Stephanie stopped at the nurses' station to leave a note for Dr. Lanman.

I woke up the next morning with a sharp cramp in my lower abdomen. I found the call button and summoned the nurse.

"Good morning, Paul," she said, hurrying over when she saw me grimace in pain. "Where does it hurt?"

It hurts around my kidneys, or bladder or something, I answered, but no words came out. Another spasm hit me, and I pointed.

"Here? Down here?" She touched my pelvic area.

I nodded.

"Okay, I'll call the resident right away." She hurried out of the room, and a few minutes later, the resident arrived.

He poked and prodded, thought for a moment, then said, "Well, this could be a bladder infection. Or it could be the good news that your bladder-control muscles have woken up, Paul. It might mean that you'll be able to control your urination now and won't need the catheter. I'm ordering some tests to have this checked out."

He looked at my chart, which was already nearly an inch thick. "I see you're scheduled for a swallowing test this afternoon. That's a good sign."

After the tests, the catheter was removed. But I wasn't allowed to go to the bathroom yet. *Why not?* I wanted to ask. I pointed and gestured, and the nurse ventured a guess.

"You're a little too weak to get out of bed every time you need to go to the bathroom, Paul," she explained, and held up the plastic urinal I was supposed to use instead. "Just call me when you feel the urge, and I'll help you with this."

This was a lot of activity for me in one morning. I was very tired. The nurse fluffed my pillow and told me to take a nap.

I woke up when my father-in-law came at lunchtime for his daily visit. Joe's office was only a few blocks from the hospital. I smiled when I saw him and gave him a thumbs-up.

"Hi, Paul. You're looking much better today. Stephanie told me that you've been sitting up and making progress. You'll be running around here before you know it."

My roommate was watching the TV. A space shuttle launch was about to take place. The view of Cape Canaveral caught my attention, and I pointed to the screen.

"I bet you want to watch the Challenger launch," Joe said. "I know how much you like the space program. This should be good. I'll turn up the volume, so we all can hear it, okay?"

I nodded, fixing my attention on the set. I watched as they showed clips of the first teacher who was suited up to go into space with the astronauts. I remembered my high school astronaut club. We'd been very lucky to have a lab that simulated the NASA controls and a space capsule. I remembered sitting at the controls and making the capsule turn at all angles. *I wonder where all of my scrapbooks are*, wishing that I had continued to keep clippings. *This launch would be a good one to add.*

On our first date, Stephanie and I had gone to the Smithsonian Air and Space Museum for the tenth anniversary celebration of the first moon landing, which I'd stayed up all night to watch in 1969. Space travel had always fascinated me. Recently, a Congressman had gone into space on the shuttle, and now a teacher, a civilian, an ordinary person was going into space. I had hoped that one day I would, too.

Joe had been chattering about the family, when the countdown finally began. He stopped talking, and we watched the launch. Suddenly, I knew something was wrong. The white plume of smoke following the shuttle had divided into two, way before the booster rocket was supposed to separate.

The announcer sounded concerned. The camera switched to the people on the ground as confusion, then realization, hit everyone. The Challenger had exploded in mid-air.

I was devastated. I anxiously tried to understand what the

newsmen were saying. I turned to Joe.

His face was ashen; his eyes red. "They said it exploded, Paul," he said haltingly. "They're trying to see if any of the astronauts are okay, but it doesn't look good." He couldn't muster his typical positive spin, seeing the catastrophe unfold before his eyes.

The Challenger exploded. I can't believe it. Just like that. One minute, it was heading into space; the next minute, it's all gone.

I touched the tube in my nose and looked down at my body. I remembered jogging around the indoor track and lifting weights at the gym. *My life exploded in an instant, too,* I thought.

"Paul, it's getting late," Joe said, slowly putting on his coat. "I have to get back to work. Are you going to be okay?"

I nodded. But I felt like I was drifting in slow motion through a very bad dream.

Finding My Voice
January 1986

"Paul, wake up," the nurse said. "The attendant is here to take you down to x-ray for your swallowing test."

I tried to follow what she was saying. I felt like I was in a constant state of just waking up, not quite clear-headed enough to catch everything people said.

"You're going down to x-ray to have a test to see if you can swallow," the nurse explained. "If you pass the test, we can take this nasty tube out of your nose," she said, touching the tube, "and you'll be able to eat real food."

Yes, yes, yes, I tried to say, happily. I nodded and gave her a thumbs-up to show I understood.

An attendant helped her lift me into a wheelchair and tie me in safely, then pushed me down the hall to the elevators. My old adventurer's spirit kicked in, and I eagerly looked around, trying to take in all the sights.

When I arrived in x-ray, the technicians maneuvered their equipment around me and finally got everything into place. I took a tiny sip from the cup they gave me. The contrast dye would be traced by x-ray to see if my swallowing muscles had regained enough control to send the fluid into my stomach instead of into my lungs.

"Good job, Mr. Berger!" one of the technicians said. "I think the doctor will be able to take your feeding tube out."

I'd passed another test! All my life I worked hard, enjoyed a challenge, did well on tests. I was starting to feel my old self coming back.

Soon after I returned to my room, Stephanie came in smiling. "The nurse is going to give you your first meal! She's bringing some equipment, just in case there's a problem."

I couldn't even remember when I'd last eaten. The nurse removed the sponge sucker from my mouth; I'd forgotten it was there. It was wet and minty and helped my mouth and throat feel less dry.

"Okay, Paul," the nurse coaxed, anxious about her task. "Be good and eat your oatmeal."

The gray gop looked worse than baby food. When the spoon touched my lips, I automatically opened my mouth, swished the oatmeal around with my tongue, then swallowed it. It was lukewarm and tasteless. But it was food.

The nurse was smiling. Stephanie cheered.

I smiled, and urged the nurse to give me more.

I remembered watching the Challenger blow up and thought how it was a metaphor for my own life. I'd lost every-thing I'd taken for granted: walking, talking, eating, bathing, being self-sufficient. Having a stroke wasn't like breaking a leg, where you're inconvenienced with crutches. My whole functional being was broken. But not my spirit. Now, I would have to work my way back from this infantile state to adult-hood. I knew I could do it.

All I had to do was set a goal and go for it.

Suddenly, Dr. King, the neurosurgeon, strode into the room with two residents. "Hi, Paul, how are you today?" he asked.

I nodded and gave him a thumbs-up.

"Good, good."

He conducted an abbreviated neurological test. "Stick out your tongue, Paul."

I tried, but nothing happened.

"I don't understand," Stephanie protested. "He just ate, and he stuck out his tongue then. Why can't he do it now?"

"Automatic reflexes, like the motions to eat, usually come back sooner than voluntary actions," he explained. "Eating is a good sign."

In a blink, he and his residents were gone.

The next morning, I awoke to my first breakfast. The atten-dant put the tray on my bedside table. "The nurse picked your meal for you last night," he said. "She'll help you with it.

Here's the menu for the day. Choose what you want to eat and leave it on the tray. We'll pick it up later."

I nodded, although I didn't understand everything he said. Seeing the food, however, made me feel good. It was one step closer to regaining my strength and independence.

A few minutes later, Stephanie stopped by before going to work. I smiled when I saw her and pointed to the tray of food.

"Hey, this is great," she beamed. "Let me help you. First, use this button to move the bed to sit up a little more."

She showed me the control. I saw words written by each button but couldn't read them. I nodded as the top of the bed lifted me into almost a sitting position. *I'll have to remember which one to push.*

After rolling the bedside table in front of me, she started to uncover the dishes and cups nestled in the various compartments of the tray. "You have juice, something that looks like oatmeal and some fruit," she said, unwrapping the silverware and sticking a straw in the juice cup.

My throat was dry, so I pointed to the juice. She lifted it to my mouth, and I took a slow, tentative sip. It was cool and sweet. I swallowed and took another sip, more confident.

I picked up the spoon and took a taste of the oatmeal.

"Look at you!" Stephanie exclaimed. "You're using your left hand like a natural! I guess when it comes to eating, nothing is going to hold you back!"

I didn't understand everything she said, but I nodded and continued to eat.

Stephanie picked up the menu, then showed it to me. I looked at the page and recognized a few words.

"Here's your chance to pick what you want to eat for the rest of the day. Lunch, dinner and tomorrow's breakfast. You even have a few choices; for lunch, you have a choice of tuna salad or chicken."

I nodded and pointed to the tuna salad.

"You want the tuna," she repeated aloud, to confirm that it

31

was indeed my choice.

Tuna, yes, yes, I thought, excited about the prospect of real food. I nodded.

"See, you check this space here," she said, using the little pencil the attendant had left on the tray. I nodded.

I took the cup of juice and, after a little maneuvering, got the straw in my mouth. I sipped, then coughed. Stephanie's eyes bugged out. I cleared my throat and swallowed. Everything was fine.

"Do you want to check off your dinner selection?" she said, pointing to the menu. "You can choose a salad or soup, chicken or meatloaf, potatoes or rice, carrots or applesauce and cake or Jell-O for dessert."

I took the pencil and marked the words I recognized: salad, chicken, all of the vegetables and cake.

"You want all of that?" Stephanie exclaimed.

I nodded. I knew what I was doing. As the days progressed, I found myself eagerly awaiting the morning menus. Planning and anticipating my meal choices became one of my favorite activities in the hospital.

Later that morning, the nurse and attendant lifted me out of bed. For the first time, I touched my left foot to the floor. "Good job, Paul," the nurse said, seeing that I had tried to stand and help. They put me in the chair just as the speech therapist arrived.

"Good morning, Paul," the therapist said. "It's good to see you out of bed." I nodded and smiled. My smile was a little less crooked each day as I regained strength in my facial muscles.

"Let's try some of these exercises," she said. "This will help in our evaluation. I think we'll be able to move you down to the rehab department soon. It's a better place to work on your speech and other therapies."

I nodded. *Thank you. I want to get this rehab into high gear,* I tried to say, but not a sound came out.

When she asked a question, I pointed to the "yes" or "no"

on her chart. She asked me to point out various animals, buildings, and other things on her form. I still had to fight to focus all of my energy to understand her and complete the test. It made me very tired.

"You did fine, Paul," she said. "I'll call the nurse to help you back in bed. See you tomorrow."

That evening, when Stephanie returned for her usual afterwork visit, I watched as she peeled off her wool hat, gloves, scarf, mittens and boots. *It looks like the weather is really bad,* I tried to say, but Stephanie didn't respond, so I tried again. *Is it snowing?* I asked. But nothing came out. I twinkled my fingers and made a motion like snowflakes falling.

"Yes, yes," Stephanie replied, "It's snowing and it's very cold. Did you see the snow out your window?"

No, no, I didn't know it was snowing. I don't know if it's hot or cold. I've been in bed and I can't see out the window. I'm stuck in this hospital room and I want to get OUT! But instead of shaking my head, I nodded at her.

"Good! I wasn't sure you could see anything out the window," she said happily.

No, no! I nodded my head again.

Then I saw her nod her head in return and realized what was wrong. I vehemently shook my head from side to side, trying to say "no." But nothing came out.

"What's wrong? Why are you shaking your head? Did I say something wrong? Did someone do something to you?"

I shook my head again. *No, no, I just wanted to tell you about the snow and being stuck in here.*

I sank back into my pillow and closed my eyes, trying to withdraw from the pain of not being able to communicate even "yes" and "no" to my wife. Up till now, I hadn't realized that I was continually mixing up "yes" and "no." How was I ever going to get through this? For the first time since I'd been hospitalized, I really wanted to cry.

"Hi Paul, how are you tonight," Dr. Lanman said, bounding into the room like an old friend. I opened my eyes and smiled.

"Good news, Paul," he said merrily. "When all the paperwork is done, you'll be moved down to the rehabilitation department on the second floor. They have a unit for their inpatients, a special activity room and all the therapists' offices right there.

"They'll teach you to dress yourself every morning. Then you'll have speech, physical and occupational therapy twice a day. You should see a lot of progress once you're down there."

I understood that I was being moved, and it was a good thing. But I didn't get all the words. I nodded and gave him a thumbs-up.

Dr. Lanman left, and a nurse came in. "It's time to get you out of bed, Paul," she said.

"Can you put him in a wheelchair?" Stephanie asked. "I want to take Paul down to the rehab department so he can see his new room. I'd like to make this transition as easy as possible for him."

"I'll have to clear it with my supervisor, and she'll call downstairs. See, he's not really allowed to go off the floor without doctors' orders for something like a test or therapy."

She helped me into the wheelchair and left the room.

"Paul, let's go see your new room," Stephanie said.

I nodded. I knew she was taking me somewhere, but I wasn't sure where or why.

She tucked a blanket around me, then pushed me out the door. I loved it! I would have agreed to anything just to get out of that room.

She wheeled me around the nurses' station and into the elevator, waving to my nurse, who was on the phone. Stephanie wasn't going to wait to be told "no" because of some bureaucratic regulation. "Two," she said, as she pushed the elevator button and swung my wheelchair around to face toward the doors.

In a few minutes, the doors opened and she pushed me out.

"Here we are, Paul. I'll just check with the nurse to see if they know what room you'll be in."

I smiled and looked up and down the hall. A few patients in wheelchairs were sitting outside their rooms. One waved at me. Automatically, I waved back.

Is this where they're moving me? I like it here, I thought.

Stephanie came back with the nurse and introduced me. I tried to extend my right hand to shake hands, but nothing happened.

"Hello, Paul," the nurse said. "Let's go for a tour." She walked down the hall, with Stephanie pushing my wheelchair. "The patient rooms are down this hall," she said, interrupting her tour to say "hello" to one of the patients.

"Can he have the bed by the window?" Stephanie asked when we got to my room. "That way he'll be forced to look over his right side out the window. I read that it's one way to help a stroke patient overcome the 'neglect' of his paralyzed side. The sooner we start stimulating Paul and talking to him across his right side, hopefully, the sooner he'll respond."

When can I move down here? I tried to ask. I pointed to myself, then pointed around the room.

The nurse understood. "Yes, you'll be moving in here. As soon as the paperwork is done."

I made a gesture of holding a pen and signing.

"Are there any forms I can fill out now to speed things up?" Stephanie asked.

"We're all set from our side," the nurse answered. "You need to call the HMO in the morning and light a fire under their administrator."

Stephanie readily agreed, not realizing this would be the first of many difficult calls to the HMO to get the benefits I was legally entitled to receive.

After breakfast the next day, an attendant came in. "Paul, the nurses thought you'd like a haircut. What do think?" He

35

pulled at his hair.

I touched my head and felt the stubble around the zipper-shaped scar. The rest of my hair was long and stringy, parted on the wrong side to cover the zipper.

The attendant held up his scissors. "Are you ready?"

Why not? I can't remember when I last looked in a mirror. I probably could use a trim. I gave a thumbs-up.

It didn't take long before he was combing my neatly trimmed hair into place. "That looks real fine," he said. He held a hand-mirror up to my face. "See."

For the first time since I was hospitalized, I looked at my reflection. I didn't recognize the face in the mirror. The green eyes were puffy and ringed with black bruises. The eyebrows and nose looked familiar, but the mouth looked wrong; the right side was droopy. I smiled at myself. Those were my teeth.

I reluctantly looked at the left side of my head. I knew it was my head, but I had to touch it to be sure. It was swollen on one side, large and roundish. I forced myself to look at the incision, turning my head to see it better. It was partially covered with hair that had carefully been combed over from the right side of my head. But I could still see the zipper of stitches where they had opened my skull to operate on the aneurysm.

This was like nothing I had ever seen before. I got a sick feeling in the pit of my stomach. *What has happened to me?*

The attendant put down the mirror. "Well, what do you think of your hair cut, Paul?"

I looked up at him and could tell he wanted me to say something nice. So I gave him a thumbs-up and a weak smile and hoped he would go away.

I sank down onto my pillow and closed my eyes. *If I went to sleep, then I could wake up from this nightmare.*

That evening, I was exhausted and having trouble getting comfortable in bed. I'd spent the day downstairs in the rehab department, and it was very tiring. Now the four pillows that were propping up my paralyzed right leg were arranged all wrong. Some feeling was just beginning to return to my hip and thigh, but it was tingly and bothersome. I was really uncomfortable.

I gestured to Stephanie to rearrange the pillows. "Okay, I'll move your leg around, but then I've got to go," she said. "They want me to bring in sweatshirts and sweatpants for you to wear when you move to the rehab floor tomorrow. And since you don't have any, I need to stop at Sears on the way home before they close."

She pushed and pulled the pillows under my leg. "How's that?"

It still felt wrong. I gestured again.

She moved the pillows a different way. I gestured again.

She moved the pillows some more. I gestured again.

She lost her patience and stuffed a pillow roughly under my thigh. "Ow!" I said.

"I didn't mean to hurt you," she apologized. "Let me go get the nurse." She ran out, concerned that she had really hurt my leg.

She returned with the nurse, who said, "Now, tell me what happened."

"I pulled his leg too hard and must have hurt him."

"How do you know you hurt him?"

"Because he said, 'Ow!'"

"He said something? He finally made a sound!" the nurse exclaimed.

Then she, too, pulled my leg. Again I said, "Ow." They cheered.

"Paul, your first word! You said something! You said 'Ow!'" Stephanie said excitedly.

I realized what they were saying. I gestured for them to move my leg again. I wanted to keep making the sound.

"We don't want to hurt your leg," the nurse said.

I held up my thumb, which had a little cut on it. I wanted

37

them to hurt me. I didn't care about the pain, if it meant I could talk again. Stephanie rubbed the cut on my thumb. "Ow," I said.

"Wait," said the nurse. "Why don't you tickle him, instead?"

So Stephanie tickled me. And I made a noise, and then another. I was excited and gasping for air. Stephanie stopped. *No, don't stop,* I gestured. *More, more, more! I want to TALK!*

She tickled me again, and another sound came out. She kept tickling me, again and again, until I couldn't breathe. I felt lightheaded, exhilarated and exhausted.

"Good job, Paul," the nurse beamed. "You'll be talking in no time! I'll leave a note for your doctor and therapist."

As sleep overcame me, I knew my voice would come back. With time to heal and will power, I knew I'd be back to normal.

Hot Wheels
February 1986

The next morning, Stephanie came to my room with a suitcase. "You're moving down to the rehab department today," she explained, "where you put on clothes, not hospital gowns."

She showed me the underwear, socks and tee-shirts she'd packed. She'd also bought a new pair of shoes, which were two sizes larger than my old ones, so I could get them on without hurting the toes on my paralyzed right foot.

"The nurse gave me a list of clothes to bring. But since you didn't have any sweatsuits, I had to buy these." She held them up for me to see. It was the first time Stephanie had done something that made me really mad.

I hated sweatsuits. I didn't have any, because I didn't want any. Didn't she get it? I tried to tell her, but nothing came out. So I gave her a hearty thumbs-down.

"What's wrong? You don't like them?"

I made a face and gave her another thumbs-down.

"Well, this is what you have to wear," she insisted. "The nurses said that all the rehab patients wear sweatsuits."

After I moved to the rehab ward, however, I saw a number of patients dressed in shirts and slacks. Obviously, we still had much to learn about getting the system to bend to my rehabilitation needs rather than sticking to their rule books. I not only hated the sweatsuits but also missed the opportunity to be taught how to dress myself in the clothing I had at home: button-down flannel shirts and Dockers or corduroy slacks.

The nurse came in soon after Stephanie left for work. "Hi, Paul. We're moving you down to your new room on the rehab floor."

She helped me into my wheelchair, while an attendant loaded my flowers, cards and other personal items onto a cart. I pointed to the suitcase, and they added it to the pile. As they wheeled me to the elevator, Arlene, one of the nurses who had cared for me before and after the surgery, came running down the hall.

"Paul, Paul, you can't leave without saying good-bye!" She kissed me on the cheek. "Congratulations, and come back and visit us!"

I smiled, *Thank you. Thank you for taking such good care of me.* "Zazazz," my mouth said.

"Another sound! Yea!" she cheered.

Early the next morning, Terry, my new rehab nurse, helped me take a sponge bath in bed. Then she pulled out clothing for me to put on.

"How's this blue outfit," she said, laying the ugly, new sweatsuit on my bed. I felt like saying, "Yuck." But then I thought, *if this will help me get better, I can put up with it for now.* So I gave her a thumbs-up.

She quickly had my underwear and pants on. Then she put my tee-shirt on my lap.

"Can you put this on yourself?"

I picked it up and put my head through the neck hole. But I didn't have a clue how to get my arms into the sleeves.

"You'll get it," she said kindly.

She pulled it off my head and showed me how to put my paralyzed arm in first, then my good left arm and then duck my head in. I pulled it down into place with my left hand. We repeated the process with the sweatshirt.

I hated the outfit, but it was nicer than a hospital gown. I felt dressed for work, rather than bed.

Stephanie arrived in time for our initial meeting with my team of therapists. Terry wheeled me down the hall, with Stephanie trailing behind.

"Good morning," the speech therapist said. "I'm sorry the others couldn't make it. This happens all the time. But Terry and I can give you most of what you'll need to know."

She sat down at the table in the small meeting room and

motioned for Stephanie and Terry to sit, too.

"Paul, you had a very, very massive stroke. The bleeding or the reaction to the surgery cut off the oxygen to your brain and killed the cells on the left side of your brain. A lot of brain cells were killed," she said, looking directly at me.

"Some people would have died from such a stroke. But because you're young and in good health, you were lucky to survive. Each year, one million people have a stroke, although less than twenty percent of strokes are caused by ruptured blood vessels, like yours. You should know that half the people who have ruptured aneurysms die from them."

She paused to see if I understood. I didn't understand all the numbers, but I knew something bad had happened to me and that now I would have to start over. I gave her my thumbs-up sign to show I was following her.

"Okay, good. The good news is that you're bright and have a lot of support," she said, looking at Stephanie. "The bad news is that the brain cells on the left side control your speech and the movement in your right arm and leg. For some reason, the commands for the right side of the body come from the left side of the brain. They seem to cross over just under the nose. The right side of the brain controls your left arm and leg and lips.

"When you had your stroke, the muscles on your right side lost their command center in the brain. So they stopped working. Even the muscles on the right side of your throat stopped working, so you couldn't swallow, or clear your throat or keep fluid out of your lungs. And you know what happened next: You developed pneumonia in your right lung.

"Virtually all of your capabilities to communicate were destroyed by the stroke, because the command center for language is also on the left side. Technically, you have what is called 'aphasia,' an inability to use language and 'apraxia,' an inability to use your mouth and tongue muscles to make words."

She paused and wrote the words on her notepad for me: stroke, aphasia, apraxia. I looked at them; studied them. These

41

were the words that would define my new life. In essence, they were my new name. But I had never seen these words before. And now they were little more than a jumble of letters.

"You have both types of aphasia. You have 'expressive' aphasia,' which means you can't 'express' yourself or say what you want to say either in 'spoken' or 'written' words. You also have 'receptive aphasia,' which means you have trouble understanding some of what you hear or read."

She stopped a minute. Both Stephanie's and Terry's eyes were reddening.

"I think your receptive aphasia is less severe, because it's obvious to all of us that you understand a lot of what you hear."

I nodded.

"As your 'speech therapist,' I have the tremendous challenge to find ways to help you to regain more of your 'understanding,' so you can enjoy listening to the TV and your family and friends. So you can start to read again. And, hopefully, to control some of the sounds you've just started to make, so they'll become real words. We have a very high mountain to climb and only a few weeks here in the hospital to do it. My plan is to push you to develop the areas that show the most promise. I don't think that when you leave here, you'll understand higher level concepts like slang words, or jokes that are plays on words. I don't think you'll be talking much, but you may be able to learn to say 'yes' and 'no' and a few other key words. Do you have any questions?"

She looked at Stephanie, who had tears running down her cheeks. Stephanie shook her head. I motioned for her to go on.

"I don't know as much about specific physical therapy and occupational therapy plans, but I can give you a general sense. Muscle control often returns to stroke patients, and many learn to walk with the help of a walker or cane, at least for short distances. Some people wear braces and slings to protect their weak feet and arms.

"Your occupational therapist will work with your nurse, Terry, on moving your arm to keep the muscles and tendons from tightening. They'll also show you ways to use your good left hand to wash and dress yourself; how to hold spoons, pens, and other things; and tricks for taking care of yourself with one hand."

Stephanie was trying to regain her composure. In a soft voice, she said, "It sounds like Paul's starting from zero, and there's so much to do in so little time."

The speech therapist nodded. "By the time we get most of our stroke patients, they're a lot further along than Paul and making more rapid progress. The only patients we see worse than Paul are the very serious car accident victims. So yes, Paul is starting from zero. And we'll do our best to get him as far along as we can before he's discharged."

I knew I was in bad shape, but I didn't believe I was as badly off as the therapist was telling us. *When I can talk again, I'll tell her how wrong she was. If she or anyone thinks I can't do it, I'll just ignore them. I'm competitive, and I like winning.*

My struggle to regain my speech was sometimes humorous. When I introduced myself to others, I didn't realize that the sound that came out of my mouth was "Chupus," not "Paul." One day, Stephanie heard me introduce myself as "Chupus" and repeated what I had said. When I heard her say it, we both ended up laughing. From that point on, it was her nickname for me while I was in the hospital. Even now, when we talk about my time as an inpatient, we refer to me as "Chupus."

In some ways, I really had become "Chupus." The man who had been "Paul" was gone. A new person was emerging; one with a deeper sense of the importance and meaning of life.

I began to realize how much I depended on my wife; how she lifted my spirits when she walked through the door; and how I missed her positive energy when she was late or couldn't stop by to see me on her way to work. I don't know if I could have made it without her.

I lost much of Paul's shyness. After so many weeks in a

hospital, you forget you ever had any privacy. And I began to reach out to others. Even though I couldn't talk, I found ways to initiate nonverbal communication and befriend strangers; sometimes with a simple wave or by pointing to what they were doing.

Before the stroke, I'd been very self-reliant and independent. Now I was forced to rely on others. But this became a good thing, because I learned to appreciate and value their support.

Joe continued to visit at lunch time a few days a week. Gary, my college roommate, visited almost every day. And once or twice a week a friend or co-worker would come with a bag lunch or a tray from the cafeteria to eat with me. On weekends, family and friends filled up the time. Stephanie's younger sister, Stacy, visited often. She had a close friend in the hospital at the same time, suffering from a motorcycle accident.

Funny things happened to me along the way. One time the nurse forgot she had left me in a certain bathroom where the call button was on the right side, and out of reach of my good left hand. I couldn't let her know when I was done, and half-an -hour went by. If Joe hadn't stopped in and asked the nurse where I was, who knows how long I might have waited. When I got over my initial anger, Joe and I had a good laugh about it.

After three weeks in the rehab unit, Stephanie and I were called in for a meeting with my rehab team. This time, all of the therapists as well as Dr. Lanman showed up. They called it a "family meeting," but it was really about my HMO.

Stephanie had already received a call from one of the therapists, advising us that my HMO was pressuring the hospital to discharge me. Stephanie had called the HMO and complained, citing chapter and verse of the law. The administrator backed down, agreeing not to count the days when I was on the neurosurgery floor receiving therapy as part of the total of sixty days of rehab to which I was entitled under my policy. Even so, it was clear that the hospital couldn't keep me much longer.

At the family meeting, Dr. Lanman led the discussion. "You've been in the hospital for more than two months, it's time to plan for your going home."

I nodded. As much as I liked the people here, I wanted to go home.

"You've made a lot of progress and will continue to make progress. I've discussed this frequently with the HMO's administration, and they agree. But this is not about what is right for Paul. This is about how much will be covered. The HMO's responsibility ends in a few weeks. I think you should go home and continue with a vigorous outpatient program."

I looked around the room. My therapists were nodding in agreement.

My occupational therapist said, "I've prepared a home assessment checklist to help you, Stephanie, in making your house accessible." She handed Stephanie a piece of paper that looked as though it had been copied a thousand times from a poorly typed form.

Stephanie blinked back tears. "I need all of you to give me some time frames here," she said. "Do you think that Paul will regain his ability to walk and talk if he has another one or two months of intensive inpatient therapy after he leaves here? We have some money set aside that we were saving for a down payment on a new house, and Paul's parents will help. We can afford a few months in a rehab hospital in Virginia, since it's a little cheaper. Do you think this is what we should do?"

"It's impossible to tell how long it will take for Paul to recover," Dr. Lanman replied. "It's likely to take much more than just two months. You should plan to go home and have outpatient therapy. There are home health agencies that will send therapists into your house. Or, if you can get Paul here, he can continue with a full five-day-a-week schedule of therapy as an outpatient."

The other therapists were nodding strongly in agreement. The physical therapist said to Stephanie, "Paul wants to go home, and you need to get on with your lives. Paul will make the same progress at home as an outpatient; maybe even more."

I liked what I was hearing. I nodded heartily. I wanted to go home.

45

"What do other patients do?" Stephanie asked.

"Other insurance sometimes pays for more time," the speech therapist said. "Some patients go to other rehab facilities out of town, where they have family. For others, their families help them the best they can with outpatient care. I agree that Paul still shows a lot of potential for improvement, and although it will take a long time, you should be able to find independent therapists who are not affiliated with an institution. Their therapy is just as good, and their charges are much lower, since they don't have the overhead."

After setting a firm date for sending me home, Dr. Lanman thanked everyone and adjourned the meeting. Stephanie took me down to the hospital cafeteria for a private dinner.

I was happy. The therapists had said I was doing really well. They all agreed that I'd be going home soon. So I couldn't understand why Stephanie was crying. *What's wrong?* I tried to ask her, but she either didn't understand me or didn't want to talk.

Finally, she let it all out. "What your doctor and therapists really meant to say is that they don't know if you'll get much better at all, and so why go into a rehab facility. This may be close to what you'll be like for the rest of your life, so we might as well get used to it and figure out how to adapt. Maybe you'll walk again; maybe. But in how many months from now? And how far? Maybe only a few steps. Maybe you'll always need a wheelchair."

The tears streamed down her cheeks. I patted her shoulder, trying to comfort her. *Why she was so upset? I knew I'd be walking soon. It was just a matter of time and hard work.*

After a few minutes, she pulled herself together. "I have a lot to do. I have to find you therapists; figure out how to make the house wheelchair-accessible; get all your equipment; and buy you a wheelchair. I'm not giving up my job, so I'll have to find someone to take you to the therapy sessions and be with you during the day."

Stephanie was efficient; about a week later, she had a

wheelchair for me. Since it wasn't covered by my HMO plan, she looked to see what the newspaper's classified ads had to offer. She found a wheelchair that had barely been used by an elderly woman, who had passed away. Her son said it was almost like new and offered it at much less than the cost of a new wheelchair.

My physical therapist suggested that she bring it to the hospital so the staff could adjust it for me and make sure it was in good condition.

"Look what I bought you, Paul," she said, wheeling it into my room. "Your very own, private wheelchair!"

I was delighted. I gestured to her to help me "transfer" from the hospital wheelchair into the new one. My nurse had started to teach her how to help me, so we'd be able to manage at home. She positioned the new chair as close to me as she could, then grabbed me under my arms and guided me into it.

This is beautiful! I thought. Look at the chrome, the shiny foot rest, the blue leather on the side. I hadn't felt this excited about new wheels since I'd bought my first car.

In the world of the hospital, wheelchairs were the basic form of transportation, as indispensable and sought after as cars. The patients vied for the "best" wheelchairs, and I often sent Stephanie during her before-work visit to get my favorite from the equipment room. When it wasn't available, my day just wasn't the same. Now, it would be different: I had my own wheelchair now.

I squirmed around in the seat. It felt good. *I'm taking it for a spin,* I tried to say, but just made a grunting sound. I pointed to the door and gestured for Stephanie to get out of the way. I wheeled out of the room and stopped to show my roommate, Bob, who was sitting just outside in the hall. *This is mine, isn't it nice!* I tried to say, then gestured to the chair and to myself.

"Is that yours?" Bob asked.

"Yes, we just bought it," Stephanie answered, walking up behind me.

I headed down the hall at top speed. To get to the nurses'

station and the lounge area, I had to turn right. I didn't quite negotiate the turn and scraped the new chair into the wall, taking off some wallpaper. I had to back up a little, but then I whisked down the hall.

I spent the rest of the afternoon showing off my new chair. I even made Stephanie take me to the neurosurgery floor, so my nurse-friends there could admire it, too.

"You really do need to get out of here," Stephanie said.

Dress Rehearsal
March 1986

As long as I was an inpatient, the insurance company and hospital said I couldn't leave the hospital grounds until I was officially discharged by my doctor. The rehab staff thought Stephanie and I should be allowed a few test runs. She was frightened of having total responsibility for me, even for just a few hours. But the staff helped me convince her to give it a try.

My first outing was a Sunday drive around the city. As the nurse wheeled me to the elevator, I waved to my new friends in the rehab unit. I was happy to be going out.

"It's one o'clock now," the nurse announced, glancing at her watch. "Be back by two-thirty, so I can get Paul settled in for the afternoon. My shift ends at three."

"Okay," Stephanie said. "It's a pretty day and we'll probably just drive around."

When the elevator doors opened, she dashed out to get the car, which was parked down the street. I looked around the lobby with my old traveler's curiosity. I'd been to other floors, and the cafeteria, but didn't remember the lobby.

The nurse stopped just inside the double glass doors. When they opened, I felt the chill air on my face, and savored it. From my wheelchair, I could see some cars, people walking and a bus. I felt a deep emptiness; I hadn't realized how much I missed the outside world.

My heart skipped a beat when I saw my car pull up to the door. It was like seeing a dear friend. I'd bought it only a few months before my stroke; after much research, consideration, discussion and comparison shopping.

Stephanie jumped out. Before I knew it, the nurse was helping to swing me from the wheelchair backwards into the front seat of the car. It was an odd feeling, going in backwards, not being in control. But before I could blink, they had tucked my legs and arms into the car and closed the door.

"Bye," the nurse waved. I waved back.

"I'll call you when we get back," Stephanie said. But the nurse had already turned and whisked the empty wheelchair back into the building.

Stephanie settled into the driver's seat. "Let's fasten your seat belt."

She reached over to help me, and I felt the buckle snap securely into the slot near my left hand. I realized I could fasten it with my left hand; having a paralyzed right hand wouldn't stop me from going out.

I looked around the car's interior and touched the cloth seat, the dashboard, the padded door, the window knob. I rolled the window down, another thing I could do myself with my left hand. I flipped the door lock closed; another thing I could do. I relaxed a little and settled back into the seat.

"Where do you want to go?"

Everywhere, I tried to say. She didn't understand, so I made a big circle with my hand.

"You want to go all around the city. Since we're downtown, why don't we start with some nearby landmarks. My dad's office is just a few blocks away."

I nodded. As we drove past buildings I recognized—Joe's office, Stephanie's office, a new hotel I'd helped to get built—I got excited. Stephanie turned down the next street and, a few blocks later, we came upon the subway center development I'd worked on. She pulled over into a loading area, so I could admire the department store and hotel that had been constructed over the subway stop.

"How does it feel to be out?"

I smiled, patted my chest near my heart, then gave her a thumbs-up.

"Good! Let's drive over to the bad side of town; to your office!"

She drove toward Capitol Hill. I saw the dome of the Capitol rising clear and white against the blue-gray winter sky.

Seeing it always made me feel patriotic and warm inside. She turned up North Capitol Street, past Union Station, the subway stop I took to work. She stopped in front of another building I'd helped to get built. My office was in the next block.

"I bet you wish you were back at work. Even though you were planning to leave, I bet you'd rather be there than in the hospital."

I agreed heartily, nodding emphatically, smiling. I wanted to tell her everything I was feeling, but only a funny-sounding noise came out. All the emotions I felt from seeing these familiar sites were making me tired. And fighting the tiredness seemed to drain my energy even more.

"You look sleepy. Do you want to drive by our house, or just go back to the hospital? We still have almost forty-five minutes and should be able to make the round trip in time."

I didn't think I would be able to appreciate it, so I shook my head. "Back to the hospital," Stephanie confirmed.

When I finally arrived in my room, I was exhausted. But getting out of the hospital and seeing the projects I'd helped build gave me hope that, if I worked a little harder, I would soon be back to my old self.

The weekend prior to my discharge was scheduled to be an all-day outing to my house. It would be a dress rehearsal; a way to ease back into my old life.

I was really excited as we drove down our block. Stephanie backed into the driveway, so my side of the car would be lined up near the front walk. That way, we avoided one flight of steps. But we still had a big step onto the porch and another one into the front door. The ramp our neighbor was making for me wouldn't be ready until later in the week.

Stephanie managed to tip my wheelchair and somehow bump and drag me up the two steps and into our living room. I sat in my wheelchair and looked around. The room looked familiar but felt very strange. The warm feeling of "home" just wasn't there.

I wanted to walk across to the dining room and look out the

window into the back yard. But I couldn't get out of my wheelchair, and I couldn't make the wheelchair roll on the thick wall-to-wall carpet. In the hospital, the floors were smooth tile, making it easy to move under my own power. But in this room, with the furniture I had selected before we were married, with the carpeting I had liked so much, I felt like a baby, waiting for someone to take me around. I tried to hide my growing despair, while Stephanie chattered on about how happy she was to have me home.

A few minutes later, my in-laws, Joe and Lila, arrived with an elaborate, home-cooked lunch. As we ate, I started to relax.

Then I heard the doorbell ring. My back was to the door, so I reflexively tried to turn around to see who was there. But the muscles in my upper body were just too weak. The best I could do was turn my head and see about half way. It was very frustrating.

Stephanie was up and answering the door in a blink. I heard her greeting our friend, Sandy. Then I heard another sound: Sandy had her four-month-old baby with her.

In another blink, Stephanie was behind me, dragging the wheelchair around, so I could face into the living room. She motioned to Sandy to sit on the sofa. "I really wanted to visit you in the hospital," Sandy said, "but I couldn't leave the baby. And I didn't want to bring her into the hospital; it just isn't safe for a newborn."

Not for me.

I looked at the little baby. In many ways, I felt just like her. My mind was active, my intelligence strong; but my body was weak, helpless, unable to go anywhere on my own; unable to talk or walk.

"She's really an advanced baby," Sandy said proudly. "She can turn over, and she's already starting to crawl a little."

I forced a smile, feeling very sad inside. I couldn't turn myself over in bed yet.

After Sandy and her baby left, I tried to help Joe assemble a new metal utility cart that Stephanie had bought for me. I was using a rolling tray-table in the hospital for my toiletries when

I dressed, and Stephanie wanted me to have the same conven- ✗
ience at home. But instead of buying an expensive piece of
medical equipment, she found something in the hardware store
that would do just as well, for a fraction of the cost. The utility
cart had wheels, so I could move it around wherever I might
need it; three metal shelves for storing all of my toiletries; and
an outlet with a long cord for my electric shaver.

I held one of the aluminum supports, while Joe screwed a
shelf into place. I remembered all the times I had assembled
things and knew I used to do this better than Joe. But now I was
getting confused just watching him. How was I ever going to
return to my hobbies or to being the man of the house if I
couldn't even hold a screw driver and assemble a simple utility cart?

Suddenly I felt totally overwhelmed. I was starting to "shut
down."

"You look really tired," Stephanie said. "Do you want to lie
down and nap on the sofa?"

I shook my head. I wanted to go home—back to the hospital—right away. Being in this house was making me feel anxious and overtired. I wanted to leave now.

Stephanie helped me pull on my coat, and we went out the
door. Her parents said they would finish, straighten up and lock
the house. She was a little clumsy getting me down the front
step, banging my legs against the door frame and my feet on
the step, but somehow she got me into the car, folded up the
wheelchair, and drove me back to the hospital. I could tell she
was stunned that I hadn't seemed happier to be at home and
that I wanted to leave so soon, but I was just too tired to
explain.

Although some wives quit their jobs to stay home and take
care of their husbands, Stephanie didn't want to stop working.
Besides, we needed her income. So she decided to hire someone to take care of me during the day.

She called home health agencies and rent-a-nurse firms,
looking for someone who would drive me to my therapy

appointments; help me with homework; and take me out for lunch, to shop, run errands, sit in the park—anything out of the house. Since she'd be out at work all day, she decided that I should be, too. That way, in the evening, we could talk about our respective days and relax together.

But that's not what these agencies are set up to do. They don't have staff to drive patients around, because insurance companies typically categorize patients either as "home-bound," and therefore eligible for the agencies' services, or "ambulatory," able to get around and, therefore, not eligible for services. The agencies weren't prepared to do something different than what the insurance companies dictated. So they told Stephanie she was "wrong."

But she knew I didn't need a nurse to sit at home with me and knit: I needed a driver/companion. So she asked her boss and the receptionist at work if it would be okay to place a "help wanted" ad in the newspaper and list her work phone number. They were anxious to help and agreed.

The ad said the person must be able to drive and to speak English. Many people were screened out by the receptionist, either because she couldn't understand their English or they couldn't drive. Eight people made the cut, and Stephanie interviewed them by phone. She insisted on checking references, and only two candidates received glowing recommendations: a young man from England, who was working as a baker and wanted more normal hours, and a young woman from Central America, who had earned a business degree in Boston and had worked as a personal assistant to a disabled lawyer. The final choice would be mine.

Stephanie arranged for the two finalists to meet me at the hospital during evening visiting hours. John came in a sports coat and was a little shy, but he told me that he wanted to help me and physically lifted my weight all the time as a baker. I liked him and thought he would be okay. We shook hands, and Stephanie said she would call him the next day with our final decision.

Then Janey arrived. She wore a frilly sundress and high

heels. Something about her personality made me feel happy, and we hit it off immediately. I liked her energy; her spirit; her business degree. ✳

My nurses and therapists thought I should select John. They thought it would be easier for him to push me around in the wheelchair, pick me up, and, as a male, be a better companion.

But this was my choice. So Janey started during my final week in the hospital; spending all day following me around and learning from my nurses and therapists how to take care of me. They told her to wear flat heels or she wouldn't be stable enough to help me in and out of the wheelchair. She didn't own any flat heels, and she managed just fine.

One of Stephanie's many fears about my coming home was that I would fall down, and she wouldn't be able to pick me up. So she spoke to my physical therapist. "I don't want to call the paramedics every time Paul lands on the floor. When he taught me how to ski, the first thing he taught me was how to fall and how to get up. Learning that really saved me in some tight spots."

"That's interesting," the therapist said. "We've never worked on that. When a patient falls, he usually has an exercise belt on to give us something to grip. Or in a difficult situation, another therapist helps us.

"Let me learn what to do and practice with Paul for the next day or so. When you come in, I'll have it all worked out and show you how."

A few days later, Stephanie came to my afternoon physical therapy session.

"Okay, Paul," the therapist said. "Let's show Stephanie what we've been practicing. Are you ready?"

"Yes." This training had been difficult, but I had enjoyed it, because I could understand its purpose.

She pushed me off the therapy table, which was about

eighteen inches above the floor, onto a mat. Even though I was expecting it, I didn't have enough control over my body to prevent myself from flopping over into a pretzel-like mess.

"Now, we move his legs and arms around, so everything is lined up like this." While I was still on the floor, she motioned to Stephanie. "Try it yourself, Stephanie, to see how it feels. Then you'll understand how to get Paul set."

Stephanie followed her lead. Then the therapist gave me a chair.

"Come on Paul, pull yourself up now, like we did yesterday."

I grabbed the chair with my good left hand, then pushed myself up with my left leg. The therapist then helped me onto the chair.

"See how easy it is. Now you try it."

She spilled me onto the mat again. Stephanie rearranged my arms and legs, then stood by to assist me as I helped myself up into the chair.

"We did it! You did it!" Stephanie exclaimed.

"Yes!" I was excited, too, and flashed my thumbs-up sign. I was really proud of myself for passing this test.

At home the following week, I was sitting on the edge of the bed getting dressed, when my sock fell off the bed. I reached for it, lost my balance and ended up on the carpeted floor with a thud.

Stephanie, who was downstairs making breakfast, leapt to the top of the stairs, scared that I'd hurt myself. I laughed and tried to reassure her that I had landed on my bottom and was okay.

"Are you sure you're okay?"

"Yes, yes." I gestured to her to move my legs around and pull the chair over, so I could get up, just as we had practiced. I pushed myself off the floor and onto the chair, without her help. Then she helped me shift to the bed and handed me my sock, so I could finish dressing.

The training paid off right away. It was obviously worth our effort to get my therapists to address my everyday problems and help me solve them in ways that would promote my independence.

Coming Home to a New Reality
April 1986

Planning for my discharge made me very happy. But it never occurred to me that I would be going home severely handicapped. I had imagined that I'd walk out to the car and, after a few weeks of outpatient therapy, head back to work. Stephanie said that she had felt the same way. Even though she'd heard the doctors and therapists say there was little hope I would regain much else after leaving the hospital, she was positive I would recover. She had even promised my boss I would return to work by the end of the year.

Finally, after three months in the hospital, my last day arrived. I was waiting impatiently in my room when Stephanie showed up.

"Are you ready to go home?"

I gave her a thumbs-up as high as I could lift my arm. Then I wrote the number "4" on my notepad and motioned toward the elevator and up.

"You want to go to the fourth floor to say good-bye to the neurosurgery staff?"

"Yes," I said, nodding. I now had a vocabulary of about ten words.

"Let's pack your things first; then you can say good-bye."

I helped her fold my clothes and put them in the suitcases. Soon we were on our way to the neurosurgery floor.

Dr. King was at the nurses' station, writing orders. I recognized him and stuck out my tongue. That's what he always asked me to do as part of his routine neurological check. He laughed.

"Paul's going home for good, today," Stephanie said.

"You've made great progress, Paul!" he said, shaking my hand enthusiastically. "Don't stop the therapy. You'll see with a little time, how much you can do. I saw this with another

58

patient: He continues to make progress even today, five years after his brain surgery. Don't stop; don't give up!"

I tried to say thank you for saving my life, but all that came out was, "Thank."

Soon the nurses had congratulated me, we returned to the rehab floor, and picked up my discharge papers. I said "goodbye" to the other patients and staff, feeling just a little sadness creeping into this happy moment.

Finally we were on our way to the car, the nurse's aide pushing a cart loaded with my belongings. Stephanie helped me into the front seat, then loaded my wheelchair and things into the back. As the car pulled away from the curb, I waved to everyone—even total strangers—like a war hero in a parade.

Free at last! Free at last!

I was stunned when Stephanie pulled into our driveway. A long, narrow, ugly wooden ramp snaked toward me from the front door.

"Mack did a nice job, don't you think?" Stephanie said proudly. Our next-door neighbor had built the ramp for me.

I didn't answer. I was still absorbing the fact that I needed a ramp to get into my own house.

"Let's go," Stephanie said, helping me into the wheelchair. She had set flagstones on top of the grass, connecting the driveway to the end of the ramp. But the stones didn't meet precisely, making it a bumpy ride.

The ramp was just slightly wider than the wheelchair, with no maneuvering area by the front door. It was difficult to open the screen door and front door and then push through.

I looked around the living room, waiting for Stephanie to bring in my things. I tried to push the wheelchair into the middle of the room, but the pile of the wall-to-wall carpet was too thick. I tried again, frustrated that I could use only my left hand and foot to propel myself. This had worked well enough on the tile floors in the hospital, but I couldn't move by myself in my own home. Luckily, it was a small house, and I was sure I'd be walking soon.

"What do you think of the stair glide?" Stephanie asked as she put down the bags and closed the front door.

I looked at the padded chair sitting on rails on the staircase to the second floor. Stephanie had shown me pictures of different lifts, and this was one of the simpler models.

"It almost didn't work," she said, as she pushed me toward the contraption. "See how our staircase goes up, then the last two steps make a sharp turn at the top? Well, this is designed for straight stairs, but the mechanic rigged it so it should work. It just means that you'll have to be careful at the top, because there's a little gap."

I nodded. It reminded me a little of a ski lift. They'd never bothered me; even ones that were difficult to get on and off.

She pushed my wheelchair into position and helped me pull myself onto the stair glide chair. Then she swiveled me around, so I was facing upstairs.

"See these controls? I had them installed on the left arm, so you can operate it yourself. Just push this, and it will take you up."

I pushed the lever and rode to the top of the stairs. The stair glide took up a little more than half the width of the staircase, leaving just enough space for Stephanie to walk up beside me. At the top, she swiveled me toward the landing. There was a fifteen-inch gap between the end of the stair glide and the last two steps. In her enthusiasm, she started to help me off the stair glide. She wasn't thinking ahead.

I tried to yell at her, and some angry sound came out. She stepped back.

"I'm sorry! I forgot to get a chair," she said, trying not to get upset. "I'll get a chair from the study."

She brought the desk chair from the spare bedroom we used as a study and placed it on the landing. She tried to pick the right spot for me to pivot out of the stair glide and land safely in the chair.

"See this grip," she said, pointing to a new, vertical metal handrail on the wall. "The mechanic installed it. He said that with a good handhold, you'll be able to pull yourself up and over the top steps."

I reached for the handrail and tugged on it. It felt secure. Stephanie positioned my feet to touch the landing, then held her breath. This was the final test of whether I'd be able to get upstairs to use our bathroom, sleep in our bedroom, live in our house.

I pulled myself up and used Stephanie's shoulders to balance myself. Then she helped me swing around and settle in the desk chair behind her. I smiled with relief, looking down the stairway and around the landing.

I remembered painting the stairwell just a few years before, standing on a ladder. We'd painted the whole inside of the house, and I had done the ceilings and the higher reaches. Now I couldn't climb the stairs, let alone a ladder. I couldn't even stand for more than an instant without Stephanie's assistance. I didn't like feeling so helpless in my own home.

To my right was the bathroom. I could see that the doorway was too narrow for a wheelchair. *How was I going to get in?*

I tried to ask Stephanie. When nothing came out, I gestured. She finally figured out what I was asking.

"The wheelchair can't fit into the bathroom," she said. "I've measured it. But since the bathroom is so small, I think that if you stand up and pivot from the chair you're in now, we can swing you right onto the toilet seat. Do you want to try?"

"Yes." I reached for her arms to help me as I pushed myself up. In a surreal dance, we swung into the bathroom, and I landed with a thud on the toilet seat. Fortunately, the lid was down!

In front of me, in the middle of our sparkling white and chrome bathtub, was a familiar monster: a brown vinyl tub bench like the one I'd used in the hospital. And dangling from the shower head was a long vinyl hose with a hand-held shower head on the end. I'd thought that once I was discharged I'd be leaving all this hospital gear behind. I hadn't really thought about how I'd manage at home; I'd just assumed I'd do everything like I used to.

Dark feelings began to close in on me. I was very tired. Maybe I'd feel better after a quick nap. I gestured to Stephanie.

"You want to go into the bedroom?" she confirmed.

I nodded.

"I'll go get the wheelchair."

She ran downstairs, folded up the wheelchair, lifted it, then put it down. It was awkward and heavy. She took off the foot rests, making it a little lighter, then tried again to carry it up the stairs. But the stair glide tracks made the stairway so narrow that she didn't have enough room. She tried to push it up, but the wheels kept catching on the carpet. She started to cry. Then she tried again and pulled the chair up behind her, one step at a time, trying with little success not to scratch the walls. Finally, she made it to the top of the stairs and unfolded the wheelchair with a rough and angry bang.

"I don't think I can carry this up and down the stairs every time you want to come up here," she said. Maybe we can buy another wheelchair to keep up here."

"No," I said, shaking my head vehemently. I didn't want another wheelchair. I fully expected to be done with this one very soon.

"Well, if you don't want a second wheelchair, then I'm only going to drag this thing up and down once a day!" Stephanie tearfully declared.

I couldn't understand why she was so upset. After all, I was the one who was completely helpless.

Stephanie wheeled me into the bedroom. I pushed the rolling utility cart out of the way.

"Remember, you helped my dad put that together last weekend? That's for your toiletries, so you can shave and comb your hair while you sit on the bed."

Yes, yes, I nodded, *but I didn't make this cart, Joe made it.* I felt like a stranger in my own house.

"Paul, wake up."

I opened my eyes, and I wasn't in my hospital room. I felt very disoriented.

"You've been napping for almost two hours. It's dinner time. Would you like to eat up here?"

"Yes."

We ate a light dinner, watched television, then got ready for bed.

It had been three long months since we'd slept together, had any privacy, any time for intimacy. We made love. It was awkward. My paralyzed right arm and leg were in the way, heavy weights strapped to my side. But the natural urges were too strong, and I felt a surge of uncontrollable passion. I think I surprised Stephanie; maybe even frightened her a little. But I was still young, and this part of me was very much alive and functioning. Afterwards, we cuddled for a little while, and I drifted off into a deep sleep.

The next morning was a test run, to see how long it took me to get bathed and dressed.

My hospital routine typically started with a sponge-bath in bed, because the nurses didn't have time to help me shower. Now that I was home, I wanted to go back to showering every morning.

Stephanie helped me get from the bed into the wheelchair, then wheeled me to the bathroom. We pirouetted from the wheelchair to the desk chair by the door, then to the toilet seat. I leaned on her shoulders while she pulled down my pajama pants so I could relieve myself. By now I was resigned to the fact that I couldn't stand in front of the toilet but had to sit like a child, with an adult fussing over me. *Soon,* I thought, *I'll be strong enough to do this like a man.*

Then, she helped me maneuver onto the tub bench to take a shower. I couldn't lift my right leg, so Stephanie had to pick it up and place it over the side of the tub for me.

I tried to turn on the water, but as I leaned forward, I almost fell. My trunk muscles were still so weak that I couldn't balance well enough to reach the faucets, just an arm's length away. I sighed. Another challenge, another goal.

Stephanie adjusted the water temperature. I used to love a hot shower. But a curious result of the stroke was an acute sensitivity to temperature extremes, both in showering and in food.

She handed me the soap and washcloth and left the room.

I rubbed the soap in the washcloth, then carefully put the soap back in the soap dish and hung the washcloth on the arm of the tub bench. I took the shower head and sprayed myself with warm water. It felt very relaxing. Then I carefully rubbed the washcloth down my body, starting at my neck and washing everything that I could safely reach. I rinsed, and having learned to say Stephanie's name, called to her.

She came in and gave me a time check: More than half-an-hour had already passed.

She lifted my paralyzed right arm so I could wash it, then scrubbed my back and left arm. She leaned over the side of the tub to wash my feet, since I couldn't bend over safely to do it myself. I ran the washcloth over my face last and had her rinse off the soap. My eyes had become very sensitive, and I wanted to be sure no soap got into them. Then she turned off the water and put a towel around my shoulders.

At that point, she looked down. The entire front of her outfit was wet.

"I'll have to remember not to dress before you finish your shower," she said, sounding a little frustrated.

It had felt nice to have a shower. I'd forgotten how much I used to enjoy it. But it was humiliating to need Stephanie's help. I tried to concentrate on drying myself and not think about my feelings.

When I finished, I said, "coffee." It was one of the first words I'd learned to say again.

"Let's get you back to the bedroom and start dressing. Then I'll bring up your coffee, okay?"

"Coffee," I said again, nodding.

Stephanie helped me into my wheelchair and pushed me into the bedroom. She held up one of the sweatsuits.

"Do you want to wear this one?"

"No." *No, no, no!* I hated them. I gestured for her to throw them away. Now that I was home again, I wanted to wear my own clothes.

Stephanie got the message. She opened the closet and pointed to each shirt and pair of pants until I nodded at a blue plaid flannel shirt and gray corduroy pants. She put them on the bed next to me, then went downstairs for my coffee.

While she was gone, I tried to put on my shirt. I had learned how to put on a tee-shirt, not a button-up shirt, because the nurses thought that pull-on clothes would be easier.

When Stephanie returned with the coffee, she tried it herself. "Damn it. I don't know why I listened to those rehab people and bought you the sweatsuits. You should've been wearing your own clothes so they could've taught you how to put them on."

She finally figured out that I'd have to put my paralyzed arm into the sleeve first, then throw the rest of the shirt over my back and catch it with my good arm. After a little struggle, I got it on. Buttoning it was difficult, though, because I could only use one hand and, having been right-handed, was still learning to use my left hand to do everything.

I had a similar problem with my pants. The corduroy didn't stretch like sweat pants. And I couldn't lift my bad leg or bend down safely to pull on the pants.

Again, Stephanie had to help me. We couldn't see any way around it until my balance was better.

"Next time, you put the belt through the loops before we put the pants on," she said, since I couldn't reach all the way around my waist with my left hand.

Miraculously, I had learned how to put my socks on with one hand in the hospital.

After all that, I needed a break. I took a long swallow of coffee and closed my eyes, savoring the taste.

When I felt restored, I pointed to my leg brace. It was a light molded plastic that extended from just under my right knee down around my ankle and three-quarters of the length of my foot. It was stiff, both to immobilize my ankle and to keep my paralyzed foot in a flexed position. Eventually, it would allow me to bear weight on my right leg and foot, to stand and take a few steps. I strapped it on with a Velcro strap, then held it against my foot while Stephanie wiggled my shoe on, trying not to jam my toes.

"Let's see if you can tie your own shoes," she said. She had a booklet from the American Heart Association on one-handed living, which showed how to lace shoes so they could be tied with one hand. She relaced my shoes and tried it first. I concentrated on what she was doing. I liked the idea of being able to tie my own shoes and was willing to try anything to lessen my dependence on her. Then I followed her lead.

"Wow, you got that really fast!" she exclaimed.

I felt great.

She had put my keys and wallet on the middle shelf of my utility cart. Now she pointed to them. I hadn't seen or needed them for the three months I was in the hospital.

"Stand up," she said, extending her arms to help me stand. "It'll be easier for you to slide them into your pocket."

She put the keys and wallet into my right pocket, then pulled them out again.

"You can't reach them there, can you," she laughed. "Here, put them in your left pocket."

She handed them to me and held me up while I carefully dropped them into my left pocket. They felt odd on that side, but they symbolized my independence. I liked that. Looking into the mirror, I felt happy to be showered, shaved and dressed in my own clothing.

Stephanie checked her watch.

66

"It's taken you two-and-a-half hours to get ready, Paul. I'm sure that, as we both get the routine down, it'll take less time. Hmm...this means we'll need to get up tomorrow morning by five-thirty to have time for breakfast before Janey comes at eight o'clock."

I didn't understand all the numbers she was saying. But I knew she'd wake me up in time, so I didn't worry about it.

Starting Over
April 1986

The next day, the first Monday after I'd returned home, I started my new job: outpatient therapy, with Janey my as driver/companion. I already felt that she was an old friend; she'd spent all of the previous week following me around in the hospital and was so easy to be with.

Looking back, the time I spent with Janey was special. She was extraordinary; a very positive, upbeat person, with boundless energy. Best of all, she could see the humorous side of almost everything. For instance, she always helped me in the public restrooms, peeking in the men's room first, and clearing it out, saying she had to help her husband. She had become so accustomed to going with me that, one weekend, when dining out with friends, she went to "powder her nose" and headed straight into the men's room. We both laughed about it the next day when she told me. Another time, one rainy day, Janey accidentally pushed me off my narrow wheelchair ramp into the bushes. I was holding an open umbrella at the time, and can imagine how silly it looked as I toppled over the side. Since I didn't get hurt, we laughed. We laughed about everything. And I think laughing was the best therapy I had.

My first appointment was at the hospital where I'd been receiving therapy as an inpatient. I had mixed emotions. Even though I felt like an outsider, it was comfortable to be with people I knew and trusted, making my transition a little easier.

In contrast, recovering my speech was going to be the most difficult, frustrating and time-consuming effort I ever undertook. Stephanie contacted everyone that was recommended to her: the Virginia Department of Rehabilitative Services, home health agencies and religious social services agencies. They all had the same response: They could provide therapists only if I was enrolled in their program; but I didn't qualify for most of the programs, because our income was too high. And those places that were willing to take our money couldn't bend their rules to meet Stephanie's insistence that some of my therapy be at home and some of it at the therapist's office. She wanted me to get out as much as possible but, at the same time, understood that I didn't have enough stamina to spend the entire day away from home. A mix of in-home and outpatient therapy would be ideal for rebuilding my strength and keeping me motivated. What I wanted didn't fit their way of doing things. In the end, it was our friend Becki who found a private speech therapist for me.

On the second day of my "new job," I met my speech therapist. Jenny put me through a battery of tests, then summarized her evaluation and treatment plan.

"Paul you've lost almost everything," she said bluntly. "Each week, we'll do a variety of tasks to push ahead on as many fronts as we can. We'll work on your reading skills, written and oral comprehension, forming words and phrases, saying names and understanding numbers."

I listened intently and noticed that Stephanie looked pleased with Jenny s plan.

"We'll start with nonverbal ways to communicate your needs. I'll teach you a series of gestures so you can get your point across. Something like this." She held her hand up to her ear, extending her thumb and pinkie, and said, "This is a telephone."

"No!" Stephanie burst in. "I don't want to waste his precious time with sign language. He's got to learn how to talk again!"

Jenny was taken aback but wasn't a push-over.

"It's not sign language," she corrected Stephanie. "Paul needs to be able to communicate, and he can't get across even some very simple ideas yet. I don't know how long it will be before he'll have enough vocabulary to express his basic needs. This is where we have to start, and we'll be working on all the other aspects of regaining speech as well."

She turned to me. "Is that okay with you?"

I was a little confused about the exchange, but Jenny

sounded professional and had been reassuring during the tests. I wanted to give her a chance. I nodded and pointed to Jenny.

"Okay, then," she said.

I had just one question. I tried to say the words, to make gestures, to write and draw. I tried and tried. Stephanie and Jenny guessed and guessed. Twenty minutes went by before Stephanie finally got it.

"You want to know how long it will take before you're back to speaking and writing as you did at work?"

"Yes," I said, nodding vehemently.

"I'm not sure that you'll make it all the way back to that level, Paul," Jenny replied. "But it's a little too soon to tell for sure. Let's see how the next few weeks go, and we'll talk about it then."

I tried not to show my disappointment as we left. In the car, Stephanie said, "Paul, don't be upset. Jenny was just giving her initial assessment. In the hospital, they thought you were going to be a *vegetable,* but you proved them wrong. Look how far you've come. Okay, so you have a long way to go, but I'll make sure you get everything you need. Janey and I will help you. We're still planning on your going back to work at the end of the year, and I'm sure by then, with all this therapy and hard work, your reading and writing and speaking will be great!"

I was tired and feeling sorry for myself. Stephanie's words didn't cheer me up. I had to believe Jenny: After all, she was the professional, and she'd said that I wasn't going to get better. So why bother with therapy at all?

"If you don't give this a try," Stephanie said, interrupting my thoughts, "you'll never know how far you can go. What other choice do you have? Every day, you make a little more progress, a new sound or something. I know you can understand what I'm saying and what's on the television better now than you could just after your stroke. It just takes time. You're tough, Paul. And you're not a quitter."

During the next months and years, many versions of this conversation would be replayed. I'd press my therapists for a date certain for my full recovery; they'd answer honestly; I'd get upset; Stephanie would soothe me. In the end, the argument that always won was: What choice did I have? My only hope for improvement was to keep working at my therapy.

The next day, Stephanie took Janey and me to meet my new private physical therapists, who'd been recommended by the hospital therapy staff. Sally was a physical therapist and her partner, Mary, was an occupational therapist. Stephanie said that this was a great combination. She thought the rehab profession was crazy in the way it splits up the body parts: Physical therapists don't work with arms, because that's for occupational therapists; yet occupational therapists also teach skills that aren't "occupational" at all, like how to dress, eat and bathe. I needed help with all of this, so it was nice to know they could provide it.

Sally and Mary examined me together. They pushed, bent, prodded, and asked me to move; all the while, having a running technical discussion of their findings. When they tried to touch my paralyzed right arm, I flinched and said, "Ouch!"

"I haven't touched you yet," Sally said with some surprise. "Does it hurt that much?"

"Yes," I said.

Sally gently touched my shoulder, working her way down my arm to my clenched right hand. It really hurt.

"They didn't treat your arm very much in the hospital," Sally declared angrily. "Look how tight it is!"

Mary probed my right arm down to my hand, agreeing. She listed off the technical terms for each of the problems she detected.

She pulled the fingers of my right hand open. "We can make a brace to keep your hand more open," she said. "It shouldn't be curled so tightly closed." She massaged my hand, then said, "Okay, Paul, now, can you make a fist?"

I squinched my eyes closed, concentrating as hard as I could. I moved my shoulder and upper arm and soon my fingers were clenched in a fist.

"Good, Paul," Mary said. "Now can you release the fist?"

She pushed on the top of my hand, but try as I might, I couldn't will my fingers to open.

"I've never seen him make a fist, before," Stephanie said. "I didn't know he could move his right arm or hand at all."

"Well, I think we can reverse the paralysis and pain," Sally said. "It's really too bad. Your arm should have been treated more."

Sally looked at the hard plastic brace on my right leg.

"This looks like something they took out of the closet. Do you know if they had a brace made to fit Paul?"

"No, I don't think so," Stephanie answered. "Doesn't that one fit?"

Sally shook her head.

"We'll special-order a brace for Paul by making a mold of his foot using a type of plaster. The new brace will provide support for his ankle and foot and start moving his leg slowly back to its original position. Paul, stand up, so I can show you what I mean."

I was trying to concentrate on what she was saying, but she was going too fast.

"Stand up Paul," she repeated. "Up, up."

She gestured and put her arms around my back to help me up. Then I caught on to what she'd said and pushed myself up to a standing position.

"Now, look at your good left foot. See how it points nearly straight forward? Now look at your bad right foot. It's turned out, pointing to the side. That's because the muscles in your trunk, hip and upper leg are so weak, they can't hold your leg in proper alignment. We'll work on making those muscles stronger. The brace will work with us, training your foot to point in just a little more. Okay, Paul, you can sit down now."

Again, she was going too fast for me to get it all.

"You can sit down," she repeated. "Down." She pointed

down and moved me gently toward the therapy platform where I'd been sitting.

"About your arm, Paul. The shoulder support they gave you at the hospital is good. We helped to promote it, did they tell you?" Sally said.

It was a padded harness that fit under my arms and criss-crossed my back. I wore it under my flannel shirt, on top of my tee-shirt.

"When you walk, it lets both arms swing loosely by your sides in a natural position," Mary explained. "You just have to be aware of your arm, so it's safe and you don't accidentally hit it on a door or piece of furniture, since you can't really control it yet. The straps hold the arm into the shoulder socket. That's the most important thing. You don't want the dead weight of the paralyzed arm to pull it out of its socket. It looks like you have a little problem there anyway, which we'll work on. One thing you can do now, is when you sit at the table to do home-work or eat, rest your right arm on the table. This is a simple way to support it."

"How long do you think Paul will need his wheelchair?" Stephanie asked, knowing that I was very concerned about regaining my ability to walk.

"It's hard to tell just yet," Sally said. "But I think you'll see slow, gradual progress. You can already stand and move a little with assistance. So, maybe in three or four months, you'll be able to walk a few steps with a cane. Maybe enough to walk around the house. Maybe you'll only need the wheelchair when you go out to appointments or shopping."

"What about climbing stairs?" Stephanie asked. "We live in a townhouse and the bathroom is upstairs. For now, I've rented a stairlift. I have a three-month rental contract. I can renew it at the end of three months, but do you think I'll need to?"

Sally looked at Mary. "We can aim for that as a goal. It might take three months to learn to climb the stairs, or more or less."

We set up my schedule for the following week. This had

73

been a good start. They talked a little fast, but I understood that they could help me get back to my old self. I liked them right away.

No Pain, No Gain
April-August 1986

Several weeks into my new routine, I was upstairs dressing when I heard Stephanie let Janey in and begin to talk about my day. I thought I overheard Stephanie telling Janey that there was some change in the day's schedule, but I couldn't hear her clearly. It really made me angry that they talked about plans for me in that way. They should've waited until I was downstairs to go over all these details. This wasn't fair. I needed to know what was going on. How could I make her stop talking?

"Stephanie," I called. But I hadn't learned how to project my voice, and she didn't hear me. "Stephanie, Stephanie." Still no response. She was too busy talking about me to Janey to hear me calling.

I became furious. I was angry about my situation: Being stuck upstairs and out of the conversation, because I couldn't get downstairs by myself. I felt utterly helpless, and they were making it worse. I hated this feeling of dependence and just couldn't hold it in anymore. I started to bang on my metal utility cart, knocking over the toiletries and yelling curses, not realizing that I was mumbling unintelligible sounds. Stephanie and Janey finally heard me and came running upstairs.

"What's wrong? Are you okay?" Stephanie gasped.

I'm really angry at you! I tried to say, but only gibberish came out. I could see her confusion and concern, but she didn't have a clue what I was saying.

I banged my fist down on the metal cart again, even angrier that I couldn't tell her what she'd done wrong. She looked at Janey, who was standing in the bedroom doorway, stunned. I banged again, then gestured angrily at both of them. Somehow, Stephanie finally understood.

"Are you mad at us, because you heard us talking about your schedule?" she asked.

I pointed at her, gesturing that she'd hit the jackpot.

"Gee, Paul, I'm really sorry," she said. "I just didn't think about it. Jenny has to wait for the plumbers to come and wants you to have your speech session at her house instead of her office. Janey and I were just talking about how much time it would leave you for lunch and... I guess we should have been talking to you."

"Yes," I nodded vehemently. I was still angry, but at least she understood why.

"I'm so sorry," Stephanie said. "I won't do this again."

"Neither will I, Paul," Janey said. "I'll always ask you first. Promise, cross my heart."

"Okay," I said, feeling a little more calm. "Down." I gestured to go downstairs. Stephanie helped me into my wheelchair and then onto the stair-climber, while Janey carried my coffee cup down the stairs.

Once at the dining room table, Stephanie started over, talking about the change in schedule for the day. I was still angry and hearing that the day's schedule was going to be changed added to my dark feelings.

The stroke made it difficult for me to be as flexible as I used to be. I remembered when I had backpacked through Europe and Central America; I never knew what the day would bring, but I didn't care. I liked a surprise: It made my travels more interesting. But now, when I was so dependent on others for every little activity, I'd lost the ability to "go with the flow."

"I know you're upset about the change in schedule," Stephanie said. "It won't give you much time for lunch before your physical therapy session. But there are some fast-food restaurants near the PT office, so you won't feel so stressed. Then you can come home and take a nap.

"Look, you know that some of your feelings are just the result of the stroke. The stroke makes your thought processes very chaotic. Janey and I do everything we can to keep things in order for you, so you're not distracted by a lot of background noise and change. But we can't control everything. It's not your fault, and it's not our fault. You'll see, as you get better and your energy level improves, these changes will get easier for you to take."

I sighed and nodded and concentrated on finishing my breakfast. I wondered when my energy would return to normal. Like a child, I needed a nap in the afternoon and went to bed early after dinner. It took almost as long to undress and get ready for bed as to prepare for the day in the morning. My head usually hit the pillow by eight p.m. Just the night before, my friend Alan had bicycled over to visit after dinner. I'd been really embarrassed when Stephanie brought him upstairs to sit on the bed and talk.

How was I ever going to return to my job, working full time and commuting? I knew that the subway was wheelchair accessible, but my office was four long, uphill blocks from the subway. Would I still need a nap after lunch? Where would I get the energy to put in eight hours of work?

I kept telling myself that I had almost eight months to get myself together. Stephanie had arranged with my office that I would return after Thanksgiving. That seemed like years away. I knew I'd be back to my old self by then. If only I could make the therapists keep to their schedules so I could get the therapy I needed.

That afternoon, after rearranging my schedule, rushing lunch and going through a tiring physical therapy session, all I wanted to do was go home and take a nap. I wanted to rest. Even more, I wanted to withdraw from the world. But Janey stopped the car by a small park near my house.

"Paul, it's such a beautiful Spring day," she said. "Look at the sun, the blue sky. I've been cooped up all winter. Let's sit in the park for awhile before we go home."

I really didn't want to go to the park, but she was getting me into the wheelchair before I could say "no." She wheeled me to the park and helped me onto a bench. The air was still a little chilly, but the sun felt good. We sat together, pointing out the new, young leaves on the trees; the green grass poking through the brown; the green buds everywhere. Birds flew around us, a squirrel ran up a tree and, at the other end of the park, some children played on the swings. I relaxed and remembered how much I loved being outside. *This is why I'm working so hard: to enjoy the sun and the trees, life's little pleasures.*

So many times, in so many different cities and countries before my stroke, I would find a bench where I'd sit and just absorb the atmosphere around me. Sometimes it was in the middle of a busy city; sometimes on a hiking trial; sometimes in a place where the scenery was very exotic. But I don't think I ever appreciated sitting on a bench as much as I did that afternoon in the little park by my house.

As the weeks went by, I thought more and more about going home to Philadelphia. I wanted to see my parents, who were always worrying about me. Also, they were paying half of my private rehabilitation expenses, and I wanted to show them my progress. And I wanted to thank my friends who'd come to Washington or called or written to me while I was in the hospital.

Stephanie and I were learning how important it is to let people know how much you appreciate them. This was something new for us: We'd considered ourselves very independent and self-sufficient and never took much time to be happy for what we'd had and for the friendship and love of our friends and families. Perhaps a benefit of my stroke was a heightened awareness and joy in the world around us.

We decided to go to Philadelphia over Memorial Day weekend. We wouldn't be able to stay with my parents, because they didn't have a ramp up the steep flight of steps to their front door or a stairlift to the bedrooms and bathroom on the second floor. Instead, they found a nice hotel a few miles away and reserved a two-room suite for us. This way we could have a party for my friends there.

By about lunch time on Saturday, we were ready to leave for Philadelphia. I was so nervous about finding accessible toilets that I made Stephanie stop whenever I saw a rest stop or gas station. I'd become accustomed to going to the toilet whenever I arrived at or was leaving a place. I moved too slowly to risk waiting until I absolutely had to go to the bathroom. Along the interstate, we found that some of the restrooms weren't wheelchair accessible, and we had to drive on. This made me even more fearful that I'd lose it in the car. It took us almost five hours to complete what's normally a three-hour drive.

My parents were waiting for us in the hotel lobby, anxious about the delay.

"We left later than we planned," Stephanie explained, "and stopped a few more times than usual. It's a good thing we planned the party for after dinner. We'll have a little time to rest and get things together before our friends come."

I was tired and gestured that I wanted to go up to the room and take a nap. Stephanie helped me into bed, then went into the next room to talk to my parents.

"We have a videotape of Paul's speech therapy session, so you can see his progress," Stephanie said. "I've noticed that it takes awhile before Paul can apply what he learns in therapy to what you hear in his day-to-day communication. That's why you have to see the tape."

She turned on the tape player. The tape began with me sitting at a table across from Jenny. First up was the number-counting drill. I was trying to relearn how to count to 20. Imagine, I had aced calculus, physics and accounting in school, and now I couldn't even count to 20! But I tried my best.

"One, two, three," I counted off, as Jenny held up her hand and gestured with her fingers.

"How many fingers, Paul?" Jenny asked, holding up three fingers.

"Four."

"Three," Jenny corrected me. "Count again, then stop at that number. Don't keep going."

I tried again. "One, two, three."

"How many?" Jenny asked, again holding up three fingers.

"Four," I answered, thinking I'd said the right number. But

79

I could tell by her reaction that I was wrong, so I tried to guess the right number. "Two."

"No, Paul. Look at my fingers. Three. I have three fingers up. This is hard for you: Three."

My mother asked, "Why can't he get the number right?"

Stephanie stopped the tape and explained. "One of the hallmarks of a stroke is what the professionals call 'perseveration.' It's like stuttering. For some reason, his word formation process keeps repeating a pattern. In this case, Paul has learned the pattern of counting, one, two, three, four, in order. He's giving the next number in the pattern, instead of the answer to the question. He'll have to learn to stop and think about what the right number is.

"Actually, Paul does okay with numbers written on paper, but the stroke knocked out the part of his communication center that deals with names and abstract words. This means that he doesn't know the names of numbers, or the names of the days of the week or even the names of the letters in the alphabet. He knows today is Saturday but has trouble telling you.

"It's like when we went to France. I can speak a little French, from what I learned in high school. But I really couldn't follow the numbers when they told us our room number in the hotel or how much something cost. I always needed to have them write it down. As soon as I saw the number in writing, I understood. Paul's like that. Thankfully, his intellect wasn't affected by the stroke. He knows what he wants to say, but like a traveler from a foreign country, he just doesn't speak the language."

Stephanie switched the tape back on.

"Okay, Paul, how many?" Jenny asked, holding up five fingers.

"Four." I could tell by her reaction that I was wrong, so I concentrated. "Five."

"Good! Now how many?" she asked, holding her hand in the same way, just turning it around so the palm was facing me.

I laughed. "Five!"

Stephanie told me that my parents chuckled. It made me feel good. I wanted them to know that while I took my therapy very seriously, my therapists and I could enjoy a little humor.

"Okay, Paul. Let's work on names," Jenny said, pulling out a little spiral-bound book of flash cards with the names of friends and family members written on them. She flipped to a card in the middle of the book. "Who is this?"

Names were a challenge for me, since all the people closest to me had similar-sounding names. I had to differentiate between Jenny, my therapist; Janey, my companion; and Joe, my father-in-law. Then there was Stephanie, and her sister, Stacy, and their brother, Stuart. As for my parents, I called them Mom-and-Dad as one word and had trouble remembering which was which; still, this was easier than differentiating between their given names, Ed and Edie.

The hardest was my own name. I stumbled over Paul, and sometimes I would say, Paulberger, running my first and last names together. It was almost impossible to say my last name alone. Our friends' babies could say their names better than I could say my own. It would've been even more demoralizing if I realized how often it came out wrong. But another effect of the stroke was not always being able to hear when I said the wrong word or sound.

Stephanie woke me up about an hour before my friends would begin arriving. I brushed my teeth and my hair and looked at myself in the mirror. I think my face was back to normal, although when I smiled, the right side of my mouth didn't pull back as far as the left. Droopy face muscles, still.

I looked myself up and down. I was ready. I felt better than I had for a long time, and the thought of seeing all my old friends gave me new energy and hope.

Stephanie and my parents were setting out snacks and soft drinks. I heard my Dad say, "Stephanie, I'm glad you're taking care of Paul. I couldn't do it." She didn't reply.

"Stephanie," I called. I needed her to help me get into the

other room. We wanted to surprise my parents by showing them how I could walk a few steps if I held onto Stephanie.

I made my grand entrance, slow and haltingly, but on my own two feet. "Ta, dah!" Stephanie said, to add flourish to my achievement. "See how much progress Paul has made! He's walking now!" She helped me sit down. "Soon, he'll use a cane instead of me!"

"That's great," my mother said. "I wish your speech would come back faster. That tape really opened my eyes."

Then someone knocked at the door. My friends were here! During the evening, they gathered around me, talking about their jobs and families and plans. I tried to tell them what I was doing, sometimes writing a few letters of a word or a primitive ✳ sketch until they either guessed what I meant or gave up. Everyone seemed happy to see me, and some who'd come to Washington when I was in the hospital talked about how much better I looked now.

Then my friend Ely told a joke. People laughed, so I laughed. But I didn't understand what he meant. Everyone was laughing, and I felt stupid because I couldn't understand him.

stroke

I tried not to get angry, but for some reason, it hit something inside. It ruined the rest of the evening for me. Stephanie noticed. After my friends and parents left, she asked, "Are you okay? You look really tired or..."

I nodded vehemently. All of the negative emotion I'd been repressing burst out. I banged my hand on the table. I couldn't pull my thoughts together to explain why. I wanted to tell her, but I didn't know where to begin. "Tomorrow," I said.

"Something happened. Did someone say something to you?" Stephanie persisted.

I nodded.

"Do you want to tell me now or talk about it tomorrow?"

"Tomorrow," I repeated. I was too tired from all the excitement of driving to Philadelphia, seeing my parents, trying to entertain my friends, and holding back my anger at not being able to understand the joke. I gestured that I wanted to go to bed.

"A good night's sleep does wonders for your mood," she agreed.

The next day, after some tedious guessing, Stephanie pieced together the scene. She'd been sitting across the room but had heard Ely. First she tried to explain the joke to me. It didn't sound funny the way she explained it.

"It's a play on words," she said. "Sometimes words have more than one meaning, and when you switch the meanings, it's funny. You used to be good at puns, before your stroke. Now that the meanings of words are all mixed up for you, it's hard for you to get most jokes. I asked Jenny about this a few weeks ago, because I noticed it before. Remember? She explained that you have trouble processing abstract words, especially slang. Janey was there, and she offered to give you a copy of the book she'd used to learn all the slang phrases when she first came here from Central America. Remember? Phrases like "pulling your leg.""

I did remember that conversation, but I had a little difficulty relating it to Ely's joke. I nodded. *Okay, so it's the stroke's fault again.*

I knew that Stephanie was trying to explain, to give me something to hold onto, to cheer me on. But I felt worse. The stroke made me feel stupid. Four months of therapy, all day, everyday, and I what did I have to show for it?

My spirits lifted a few days later, when my physical therapists graduated me to using a cane. I could walk a few steps around their treatment room, leaning on the cane instead of on another person. I was a little shaky, but it felt great.

For the next three weeks, I worked with my physical therapists to master walking with a cane. Then they sent me to buy my own. I wanted to shout from the rooftops: *Free at last from the wheelchair, from depending on other people. Free at last!*

Stephanie took me to the medical supply store where she had purchased my tub bench. I'd never been there before. The variety of equipment was amazing, as were the prices. I had no idea how much new wheelchairs cost and for the first time really appreciated Stephanie's finding me a used wheelchair in perfect condition.

Since I expected that I'd soon be leaving the wheelchair behind for good and that the cane would be with me all the time, I wanted to be very careful to choose just the right "look." There were simple wooden canes, carved ones, brown and black canes. They all reminded me of *old* people. I wanted something modern, something young, something appropriate for a thirty-six-year-old. Chrome was more my style.

I found a simple aluminum cane that looked almost like chrome. I managed to stand up from the wheelchair by myself, then walk a few steps in the store with the cane. It felt a little different from the one I was accustomed to using during my physical therapy sessions, but it was nice.

"Congratulations," Stephanie said, as she wheeled me to the counter to pay for it. "All you need is a knife or gun hidden in the bottom and you'll look like James Bond!"

I laughed, but it wasn't a bad image. This cane was the beginning of a new phase in my recovery. I was feeling light and free and as though I could hop around the world.

"The last time I saw you this excited, was when I brought your wheelchair," Stephanie said. "You're like a teenager with his first car."

I nodded. I was happy. I was ready to celebrate.

The next day, I asked Jenny when she thought I'd get my speech back. She showed me how much progress I'd made: I had new, expressive gestures for most of my needs; my reading level had advanced a few grades; I could write many more words; I could say about twenty-five words out loud. But I pushed her to tell me when I'd be able to speak and write well enough to go back to work.

"Paul, that could be a very long time," she said. "You're getting better, and I'm sure you'll continue to improve. But at this point, I don't think you'll get back one hundred percent.

I'm not sure you'll even get back fifty percent."

For the first time, I understand every word she'd said, and it hit me like being punched in the stomach. I could hardly breathe. For the rest of the day, I moved in a dark fog. The more I thought about what she had said, the more depressed and hopeless I felt.

By the time Stephanie came home that evening, I'd worked myself into such a depression that I couldn't talk at all. After much guessing, Stephanie got that it had something to do with Jenny and immediately called her at home. I could tell that Stephanie said some angry words to Jenny, then listened for awhile.

After the call, Stephanie told me not to ask questions about when I'd recover. For what seemed like hours, she talked about everything she'd read about recovering from a stroke, how young I was, how far I'd come, how the doctor had thought I might become a "vegetable."

"And you're not a broccoli, now, are you?" she said. I had to laugh at that.

"Paul, you have a choice. Do you want to stop the therapy?"

"No," I said. Therapy was my only hope, and I had to stay focused on my goal, no matter what the professionals said.

In early August, Sally came to my house for the first in a series of in-home physical therapy sessions to teach me to climb the stairs to the second floor. The lease for the stairglide would be up in a few weeks, and instead of extending the lease, I wanted to send the equipment back.

I'd been practicing climbing stairs at Sally's office, where she had a set-up with four steps. I was feeling much more confident, stronger and better balanced. With my cane, I was able to walk short distances from the car and around my house. I still needed the wheelchair for longer trips, like shopping, but it would only be a matter of time before I could leave it behind too.

It was a difficult session, because we had to work around the stair glide, which took up half the width of the staircase. The two new handrails Stephanie had had installed on both sides also narrowed the way a few more inches. I needed more room than normal to climb the stairs, since my weaker right foot turned out, and Sally wanted to spot me by holding onto my belt. I had to lean over the stair glide tracks to reach the handrail going up. Because I had the use of only one hand, I had to carry my cane by hooking it onto my collar, the way movie stars wear their sunglasses. It was awkward, but we managed to climb to the top.

Then we tackled climbing down, which was much harder. I hadn't realized how difficult it would be to control my weaker side going down. The cane dangling down my front was also a distraction. It was very slow going and a little scary, looking down the long staircase.

Sally taught me to hold the railing tightly; then, keeping my weight on my good left foot on the upper step, I carefully reached out with my weak right foot, bending a little, until I could feel it touch the next step. Then I shifted my weight onto my right foot and quickly moved my good left foot onto the same step.

At one point, I didn't give myself enough room for both feet and, as I tried to readjust my footing, I almost lost my balance. It was lucky that Sally was there to steady me and guide my foot into the proper position when I took the next step down. When I reached the bottom, my adrenaline was pumping with the physical exertion and excitement. I knew then that we would be sending back the stair glide and that, with time and therapy, I would be back to my old self.

System Failure

August-October 1986

"We need to start planning for your return to work," Stephanie said to Janey and me one morning. "I want Paul to get evaluated by the Department of Rehabilitative Services. They have vocational counselors and support services that can help him and his boss make the adjustment.

"Before Paul came home from the hospital, I talked to one of their counselors. We didn't qualify for any services at that time, but they said they could help in returning to work when he was ready. They said that it takes about a month to schedule an appointment and weeks after that to do an evaluation. So, if Paul starts now, in August, we should have all this finished in late October."

This sounded very reasonable to me. "Yes," I agreed.

We started the process that day, when Janey and I went to the DRS office to pick up the necessary forms. They wanted a copy of my medical records as proof that I was disabled. This seemed like a lot of unnecessary paperwork: *Just take one look at me, and you can see I'm disabled!* Notes from my doctors and therapists on my current progress were also needed. It took about two weeks for Janey and me to collect the medical records and drop the paperwork off at the DRS office.

Meanwhile, Stephanie called my boss, who said he'd do whatever it took to help me get back. He was very complimentary about my work and seemed willing to give me what I needed. She also called the personnel office and asked to speak to their coordinator for disabled persons. The personnel manager had never heard of such a thing and said she'd check with the city government's central personnel office.

Eventually, a disabled persons' representative was assigned to me. He warned Stephanie that, in most cases, the disabled person ended up leaving his or her previous job, because the city government rarely made the kind of accommodations that were needed. He said that he'd do what he could to help, but he wasn't very optimistic.

After Stephanie had hounded the Department of Rehabilitative Services for more than a month, with numerous calls and messages, my first appointment with a counselor was scheduled. The DRS office was in an older government building, with the handicapped parking some distance from the door. The pavement was poorly maintained, uneven and a little difficult for me to walk on. Because we'd left the wheelchair at home, I had to hold onto Stephanie for balance until we got into the building.

We took the elevator to the second floor, where Stephanie signed us in. We were a little early for my appointment. We waited and waited. About half an hour later, the counselor was ready for us.

The counselor called me a "client," trying to make me feel special. First she asked me some questions to verify the information in my application. I was able to understand most of what she asked and answer appropriately. Sometimes, though, Stephanie had to translate for me, either explaining what the counselor was saying or giving a more complete answer for me when I just couldn't find the words.

"Well, do you think you can help us?" Stephanie asked. "Paul just needs your evaluation of his current work potential. Our plans are for him to go back to work three days a week, just after Thanksgiving. He'll continue therapy on the other two days, for about six months or so."

"You don't qualify for us to cover your therapy," the counselor said sternly.

"Why?" I asked.

"Your wife makes too much money. And you own your own home."

"I know we don't qualify for DRS rehab services," Stephanie said. "We just need your help in making Paul's transition back to work a smooth one."

"I can't do anything for a client without a complete evaluation," the counselor said. "And if he already has a job to go back to, I don't see that you qualify for our services either."

"I understood that anyone who had a permanent disability like Paul's was entitled to an evaluation," Stephanie insisted.

"I'll have to check on that," the counselor said. "An evaluation means opening a case file."

"Well, then, open a file!"

"But if we open a file, we have to follow through with actions to complete the file."

"So it will be very easy for you, since all you have to do is open the file, evaluate Paul, give us some guidelines on what job functions he'll do best, and give us a report. The most you'll have to do is talk to his boss about making accommodations."

"I'll have to check with my supervisor." The counselor looked over my paperwork. "You seem to have all the required materials here. Please sign this form. I'll need it to open your case file, if my supervisor agrees."

I looked at the form. Stephanie said that it was a standard agreement to take a job if an appropriate one was found. "We've found you a job, so that part is easy," she said.

I signed it, looking at my sprawling letters. My signature looked like a grade school student's handwriting. I'd had a crisp, manly signature before my stroke. My new left-handed signature was so different that Stephanie had insisted I go to our bank and have the branch manager witness my signing new signature cards for our checking and savings accounts. She didn't want any challenge when I was able to write checks again.

That was the end of my first appointment. I was a little stunned when the counselor showed us out. In all, I thought it had been an odd way for someone to treat a "client."

During the ride home, Stephanie fumed. She said that she, herself, would call the supervisor to make sure I got my evaluation.

Almost three weeks later, after another round of Stephanie's hounding, the DRS called to tell us that I'd been scheduled for a complete evaluation the following week. I was really angry that I'd been assigned an appointment time without having been asked whether it was convenient for me or not. With less than a week's notice, my therapists were unable to reschedule, and the disruption ended up killing the whole week for me.

On the day of the evaluation, Janey took me to the building and helped me up to the second floor. It was nine a.m. The counselor told Janey to leave and not come back until three p.m. She was a little taken aback, but she told me that she'd go shopping until it was time to pick me up.

The counselor ushered me into a testing room. She explained that there was no right and wrong answer and that she'd record the time I took to complete each unit.

She gave me a written test and read the instructions aloud. I didn't understand and gestured for her to repeat them. She repeated the instructions slowly and showed me how to do the sample question.

I concentrated all of my being on that piece of paper. I recognized many of the words and carefully worked my way down the page. This was so important, and I wanted it to be perfect.

I changed one of my answers. It didn't look right, so I changed it again.

"Paul," she interrupted me. "I think that I'll let you finish this, we just won't time you."

I looked up and said, "Thanks." Then I continued to puzzle down the page. I finally finished more than an hour later.

"Take a break, Paul," she said.

"Coffee?" I asked.

"You want some coffee?" she confirmed. "It's across the hall. Just leave a quarter in the box."

The coffee tasted terrible, but I savored its warmth.

I didn't know if I got those questions right, and I was worried about the rest of the day.

Then the counselor called me back. This time, she had a large metal box on the table. It was painted green; not a bright green, more like a dried leaf green, but so green that it distracted me. Geometric shapes were punched out of it.

The counselor showed me a tray of blocks and instructed me to place each block into its matching hole. I was confused, because I couldn't see what this had to do with assessing my work potential. I'd thought she'd give me computer tests and office-work tests. I took a deep breath and carefully placed each block in its respective hole.

The other tests were equally humiliating. When Janey picked me up at the end of the day, I was too depressed to explain why.

"You look terrible," she said. "Are feeling ill? You look gray."

I just closed my eyes. I couldn't answer.

☞ A month later, again after Stephanie's constant hounding, the counselor read parts of the evaluation to her over the phone, since it was being typed at the time and not likely to be mailed for a few days. Her bottom line was that I did not demonstrate the ability to participate in "competitive" employment. She told Stephanie that I couldn't alphabetize or put things in numerical order. She didn't think I could do any office work.

When Stephanie told me the news, I was shocked. She was really angry, too.

"This was a stupid waste of time!" she yelled. "This is no help to your boss! What are we going to do?"

She called my speech therapist, Jenny, while I listened on the extension.

"Paul's vocational counselor said that Paul can't even alphabetize letters appropriately! I thought he was doing better than that. Was I fooling myself?"

"No," Jenny said, sounding stunned. "Did she give you any details?"

Stephanie read from the notes she'd made in her ever-present spiral notebook.

"That's not true," Jenny said. "Paul can put things in alphabetical order. He can do a lot more, too. I think that he can do a lot of office clerical work. Give me her phone number and I'll call her tomorrow. Maybe she didn't understand how to administer these tests to a person with Paul's speech problem. They don't see a lot of clients like Paul. Most stroke survivors are near retirement age and don't try to go back into the workforce."

"Thank you," Stephanie said.

"Thanks," I said.

After we hung up, Stephanie and I looked over her notes again.

"We can't send this to your boss," she said. "He won't know what to do with it. He's guaranteed a job for you, and he knows it won't be what you left. At least not right away. He's assigned your projects to another project specialist for the time being anyway. And he said that he had lots of odds and ends for you to do until you've recovered your old skills.

"What a stupid waste of time. I feel like writing a nasty letter."

I didn't know what to do, but I didn't think that a nasty letter would help. "No," I said.

That weekend, my friend Alan, who worked with me in the city department, bicycled over to visit. He pointed out that the city personnel office wouldn't care what the Virginia DRS counselors said, because they're in different jurisdictions and the one has no authority over the other. He said that it was too bad that DRS couldn't help; in fact, it sounded like they could hurt my job prospects. He suggested that we keep the DRS counselors away from my boss and my personnel officer, and we followed his advice. That was the end of my "client" relationship with the DRS counselor. Instead, Jenny served as my official ambassador, translating my abilities and needs to my boss and helping my coworkers feel comfortable with me.

Returning to "Normal"
November-December 1986

By November, I had made good progress. I could walk a few blocks with my cane, and my overall stamina was much better. I decided to donate my wheelchair to a local charity.

My speech was still so poor that sometimes I felt that they had cut out my tongue. But I had learned many new words and was getting better at making the right sounds.

So, when Stephanie found out that she had to go to New Orleans for a business meeting, we made arrangements for me to go, too. We also had Janey come, to help me around while Stephanie was working.

This would be my first "real" trip since my stroke. I enjoyed the anticipation as much as the experience, itself. Just thinking about it was a great source of motivation when the drudgery and pain of my daily speech and physical therapy sessions got me down.

When we arrived at the airport for our flight, I found myself completely confused. I couldn't understand the numbers of the flights or gates being announced over the public address system. I looked at the departure board, but there was too much information for me to sort out. So I just followed Stephanie and Janey.

Stephanie had arranged for us to board early, because I still walked very slowly. When I finally reached my seat, it was a little awkward trying to stow my cane, which just barely fit into the overhead compartment. Then trying to negotiate into the economy-class seats was an ordeal. My weak right side made it very hard to maneuver, and the stiff plastic brace that kept my ankle in place didn't bend, making my leg uncomfortable.

But I forgot all about my discomfort once the plane took off. I was in the air again; setting off on a new adventure. I felt great, like I was getting back a part of my old self.

During the next week, after Stephanie left for her meetings,

Janey and I followed our own agenda. First we had breakfast, then drilled through my speech and physical therapy exercises, then explored New Orleans. It wasn't easy, but I was up to the challenge, and my reward was that I got to know the city.

We took the trolley down historic Charles Street, with Janey and the conductor pushing and pulling me up onto the high steps of the trolley. We walked slowly around the French Quarter and, naturally, we had very nice lunches.

I talked to the waiters, shop owners and other tourists we met. Smiling, pointing, gesturing and saying the new words I had relearned helped me feel connected to the people and the place. Before my stroke, I'd found it hard to speak to strangers. Ironically, now that the stroke make it hard to speak, I wanted to talk to everyone. The nice part was that most people were very pleasant, especially when I smiled and laughed at myself if I couldn't say the word. If they had time, I'd write a few words or parts of words in my pocket notebook, so they could puzzle out what I meant.

Going in and out of our hotel was difficult. It was an older building, with stairs at every entrance. None of the stairs had handrails, so I had to carefully place my cane on each step and hope I could keep my balance, or hang onto Janey or Stephanie. Later, I had Stephanie write them a letter strongly suggesting that they install a ramp or handrail.

In the evenings, when Stephanie finished work, the three of us went out to dinner. The food was great, and you could hear music everywhere. One night, toward the end of our stay, Stephanie and I were too tired to go out, and not very hungry. Janey decided to get some beignets, the special doughnuts that New Orleans is famous for. She was gone for an hour and a half. When she returned, she told us about the long line in the little store and all the people in the street. She had us laughing at the little bag of beignets she had to show for her effort.

A week after the trip, we celebrated Thanksgiving at Stephanie's parents' house, with her big family. Everyone was touched by the feeling that the year had been truly special; that this Thanksgiving, we really had a lot to be thankful for.

The following Monday, December 1, was the day Stephanie had arbitrarily chosen for me to go back to work. My boss had agreed to let me return on a part-time basis, so I could continue my speech and physical therapy.

That morning, I got up early, showered, ate breakfast, and put on a suit. My mother-in-law had figured out how to tie a tie with one hand and taught me how. But I was too nervous to do it myself, so Stephanie helped me.

She took the day off from work to come with me and help smooth the way. I really didn't think I would need her; I had a mental image of walking through the door of my office building and having everything be the way it was before my stroke.

I had asked for certain accommodations for my disability, which were provided. I needed a private office, because I couldn't concentrate in the noisy environment of the open "pit," where my desk and files had been. I was also allowed to have my speech therapist come in once a week at lunch time for a session.

My coworkers greeted me kindly, with warm and welcoming comments on my return. My boss seemed just as nervous about my return as I was; maybe more so. He wasn't sure what my new responsibilities would be, but he was willing to give it a try. And his boss, the department director, watched over me like a guardian angel.

One of my first tasks was to get a document copied for a coworker. Stephanie followed me down to the copy center in the basement. I remembered to fill out a work order, trying to write as clearly as I could with my left hand. Stephanie held the paper so it wouldn't slip. The copy clerk recognized me, and greeted me warmly. It felt good to be working again.

When I returned with the copies, my boss gave me a memo to read and analyze. Before my stroke, I had spent most of my time either writing memos or analyzing and summarizing documents for my boss. This was something I was very good at.

I looked at the memo he'd handed me. I tried to read it, but it looked like it was written in a foreign language. I recognized a few of the words, but I just couldn't put it all together.

Stephanie pointed to a line on the first page. It indicated that I had written the first draft! Until that moment, I had thought that I still could do my old job. I was stunned. Now I didn't know what I could do.

"There are lots of things you can do," Stephanie said, trying to cheer me up. "It's just your first day back. Give them a few days. I'm sure they'll give you computer work to do."

A few months previously, Stephanie had purchased a used computer from one of the new section chiefs in the department. She'd taken it to a small store in our neighborhood and had it upgraded so I could run speech therapy software as well as office programs. I'd been practicing Lotus 1-2-3, which I'd used at work before my stroke.

Once I got settled, here's what I did at work: I typed schedules of various city land development projects; I typed a list of developers and other contacts for the department; and I sorted through and organized numerous project files. In addition, my friend Alan found a task for me that no one else wanted to do: filing each week's legal notes in their respective notebooks.

I didn't mind doing these clerical tasks for the time being, since I wasn't up to writing memos and giving reports in staff meetings. What made me mad was that this was exactly the kind of work that the Virginia Department of Rehabilitative Services counselor had said that I couldn't do. This was proof that their testing method was irrelevant and hurtful. Each time I completed a task, it felt like revenge on the DRS counselor. It was a strong motivator for me, both then and now.

To fill up the rest of my day, I did my speech homework. I also completed math problems. Stephanie had found computer software for school children that created worksheets of math problems. Each week, she printed out a dozen worksheets for me, so I could practice addition, subtraction, multiplication and division. The answers were printed at the end, so I could check my work. Most of the time, I scored ninety to one hundred percent, even as Stephanie increased the difficulty levels. This made me feel great: At least I hadn't lost my math ability.

Another bonus of returning to my old office was being around more people, especially other men. I hadn't realized how much I'd missed them during the past year. The men made jokes, treated me like a man and didn't pamper me. Once a week, the other project specialists would include me in their lunch plans, usually walking a few blocks to a nice cafeteria. They were a little impatient with how slow I was, not realizing that I was pushing myself to try to keep up with their pace. But I always enjoyed that time, listening to their stories; sharing their complaints about the bureaucracy; finding ways to communicate with them by smiling, nodding, gesturing, saying a few words and writing out others.

In almost no time, it was New Year's Eve. One year had passed since the aneurysm had ruptured my life. Our friends, Jerry and Marie, who had planned to be with us the previous year, made the trip from Philadelphia to celebrate with us. We had a wonderful time.

I don't remember when I had ever been so happy to bring in a New Year. I had survived the worst year of my life and was well on my way to achieving new goals. I was walking, talking, reading, writing and working again. Although I wasn't satisfied with my level in each of those areas, I had concrete plans to achieve my goals. I felt like the Paul Berger I remembered: always striving to do more, to do better and to push forward.

Part 2:
Exploring My New World

Have Cane, Will Travel
1987

One day, after lunch at my desk, I took a walk around the block. As I hobbled around the back of my office building, two men came up behind me. I didn't hear them coming or see their faces. I think one stuck his finger or maybe a gun in my back and told me to give him my wallet. I said, "Okay," and gave them my wallet. They grabbed it and ran away before I could see anything. Upset and shaking, I walked as quickly as I could with my cane back to my office. I had been mugged before, but I couldn't believe it had happened again. At least they ran away and didn't hurt me.

When I reached the third floor, I went into the office nearest the elevator, Bill's. I didn't have words to explain what had happened, but he could tell something was very wrong by my anxious gestures. I pulled out my empty pocket to show him that my wallet was gone.

"Those cowards," Bill said, as he called the police. "Cowards to steal from a handicapped guy with a cane. How much money were you carrying?"

I knew it wasn't much. I wrote down $15.

I thought to myself, *That was pretty dumb on my part.* I knew my office was in a bad neighborhood, but I had walked around the block by myself before, without feeling afraid. And I didn't think of myself as being handicapped or an easy target. I still saw myself as I used to be. I realized then, for the first time, that I could have easily been knocked down. If they had hurt my good arm, I would have been helpless.

"Credit cards?" Bill asked, as he spoke to the police.

"Yes."

"I'll call your wife for you," Bill said, "so she can cancel your credit cards and replace anything else."

By the time I got back to my desk, everyone in the building seemed to know about my mugging. Their concern and support made me feel a little better. But the mugging was a miserable reminder about how vulnerable and dependent I was. I really needed to feel more independent.

An important measure of independence was being able to drive again. Stephanie had insisted that I wait for the winter weather to end before attempting to get behind the wheel. As soon as the first signs of Spring appeared, I contacted a driving instructor who specialized in helping handicapped drivers return to the road. His car had two steering wheels and two sets of pedals, so he could take over control of the car if necessary. He also had the special adaptations for one-handed driving. I signed up for three lessons, one per week.

The first day out, I drove around the neighborhood. It felt really strange to use my left foot on the gas and brake pedals. I felt like I didn't have control of the car. I got so tensed up from the experience that I could hardly bend to sit down when I got home. From the shocked expression on Stephanie's face, I knew I must have looked even worse than I felt. But when she questioned the instructor, he said that I'd done fine and would see me the following week.

I was flooded with conflicting emotions. On the one hand, I so much wanted to drive that I would have walked through fire to do it, which is exactly what I felt I'd just done. On the other hand, I wasn't sure my left hand and leg were smart enough to figure out how to drive. It had felt so strange and awkward.

During the second session, I felt a little more relaxed. I drove to all the places that were part of my normal routine: the grocery store, laundry, library and therapist's office. I felt the car responding to me. Although I was stiff from nervous tension when I returned home, I knew I'd soon be driving my car again. It wouldn't be long before I'd regain my independence.

My third lesson was a road test. It would let the instructor decide if I needed more lessons. He had me drive down Route 50 to the Beltway, then return home via Interstate 66. It was all high-speed driving, and I was a little nervous. But I felt a lot more in control and, when we got home, he announced that I was ready to drive on my own. He told us how to outfit my car, with a knob on the steering wheel to give me a solid grip and a u-shaped pedal extending the gas pedal to the other side of the brakes, so I could use my left foot on it, like the one in his student car.

I was so happy, I couldn't wait. I bugged Stephanie until she called the mechanic at home that evening. He told her it would be a few weeks before the parts came in. To me, it felt like forever; like a prisoner counting the days until my release.

Being able to drive again was really a boost to my manhood. Instead of being chauffeured around like a little kid, I could go places and do things all by myself. Even more important, Stephanie began to take my driving for granted, just as she had before my stroke. In fact, I remember the first time she really depended on my driving ability and how great it felt to have her rely on me for a change.

It was the following Winter, and there was a terrible snowstorm. From her office, Stephanie had taken the Metro to a subway station within a few miles of where we lived. When she arrived, however, the bus that normally would have taken her the rest of the way home wasn't there. The storm had disrupted all the bus schedules, and things literally were a mess. She tried to call me to pick her up, but I was still at my therapist's office. As luck would have it, when I finished my session, I'd decided to drive straight to the subway stop to see if I could find her. Sure enough, there she was on the corner, waving for a taxi. Boy, was she glad to see me! "You're my knight in shining armor!" she exclaimed.

But that's not to say that driving one-handed has been easy. Until I got the car I have now, the car's steering wheel used to lock up whenever I accidentally bumped it getting in or out. To unlock it required turning the key with one hand while turning the steering wheel with the other, a feat I wasn't capable of performing.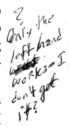

Stephanie typed up a notecard for me, explaining the problem. That way, if she wasn't home when I wanted to go out, I could show the card to a neighbor, who would then help turn the wheel. What we hadn't counted on, though, was the wheel's locking up when I was away from home. Unfortunately, one time it did. When I tried to get other shoppers to help me, they avoided me like I was some kind of criminal. Finally, after I'd flagged down about three people, someone did help me unlock the steering wheel. Later, I figured out a way to jam my left leg up into the steering wheel to move it, while I turned the key. And the car I have now works differently, so I don't have to worry about finding help to turn the wheel.

One day, of course, the inevitable happened: I was in heavy traffic on the Beltway, not going very fast, when the fourth car behind me was hit by a truck. I became part of a chain reaction that jolted the rear of my car, bending my car's fender and part of the trunk. Along with everyone else, I pulled over to the shoulder and waited for the police to come. I was nervous about how the police would treat me, since I was obviously a handicapped driver. But when the police officer came over to me, I didn't have to say much; I showed him my driver's license, car registration and insurance card. Then I was given the truck driver's insurance information and told I could go. It turned out not to be such a bad experience after all.

I felt even more independent when I made a breakthrough in regaining my speech. Up to this point, my progress had been like digging through a mine: I chipped away little pieces at a time, and it was only when I stopped to review my progress that I could see how far I'd come. Inside my head, in my thoughts, I knew what I wanted to say. But I just couldn't make the right noises. The stroke had wiped out the part of my brain that remembered how to make sounds into words.

Relearning how to make the sound of each letter of the alphabet was a magic key to unlocking the door to my brain's word factory. Jenny, my speech therapist decided to try a method that's used for teaching hearing-impaired children to speak: a set of picture cards of the mouth, teeth and tongue that shows where to place your tongue to make each sound. First I'd touch the inside of my mouth or the back of my teeth to feel where my tongue should go, then I'd look in a mirror to see if my lips were in the right position. For instance, my mouth had to be rounded for an "O" or stretched back in a smile to make an "E." At home, I practiced each sound in front of a mirror until I got it right.

Because of my stroke, I also needed help remembering what sound each letter of the alphabet represents. So, just like toddlers learn "A is for apple," I had my own personalized cues, like "cane" for "C," "tea," Jenny's usual drink, for "T" and my favorite, a power fist in the air, representing the upbeat attitude of my father-in-law, Joe, for "J."

To sound out a word, I'd line up the cards for each letter and then pronounce each sound according to the instructions on the card. Once I'd sounded it out, I tried to say it faster, making the sounds run together to form a word. Gradually I moved from one-syllable words, like "cat," to more complex words, like "industry." I tried to visualize each syllable of the word, like "in" (my coffee mug), "dust" and "tree," so I'd be able say "industry" without needing the letter cards. Then I'd practice repeating the word over and over, for many weeks. Even then, though, the odds were only fifty-fifty that I'd say the word I had in mind.

As you can imagine, this complex and tedious process could be very frustrating for people who were listening to me. The worst part was when someone tried to speed things along by finishing the word for me. This interrupted my thought process for retrieving the word and made me angry. Stephanie would get upset when I got mad at her and said that I insulted her or embarrassed her in front of others. I didn't want to hurt her, but even though I usually kept myself calm and upbeat, sometimes my disabilities got to me. After taking a break or having a good night's sleep, I'd feel better. And I would remind myself that I had come a long way from that day in the hospital when the only word I could say was "Ow!"

My routine of part-time work and continuing speech and physical therapy was physically and emotionally draining. My progress was measurable, but so very slow. The tasks I was assigned at work were boring, but my reading, writing and speaking skills weren't up to a level that I could do any more challenging work. I started to feel depressed. I needed something to look forward to. So we decided to take a trip at the end of the summer. Knowing that I'd be traveling in a few months helped my attitude improve and gave me some positive motivation. I didn't care where we went, I just wanted to go somewhere new and different.

Given the success of our trip to New Orleans the previous Fall, we decided to try a trip outside the U.S. After looking through a variety of travel brochures and guidebooks, we decided on Ireland. We'd never been there before, and there were several points in its favor: We wouldn't have to deal with a foreign language; Stephanie could drive us around at our own pace; there was an extensive bed-and-breakfast network; and it fit within our budget.

A few years later, I learned how concerned my doctor and therapists were over this trip. People just didn't think that you could travel if you had disabilities like mine. But I enjoyed the challenge.

Before my stroke, I had done most of the planning and arranging for our trips. This time, however, because of my poor speech, I had to rely on Stephanie to do most of the legwork. The Irish Tourist Board sent us a lot of good travel information, including a book with photos and detailed descriptions of numerous bed-and-breakfasts. On the basis of the pictures, we selected modern-looking one-level guest houses that offered a private bathroom. That way, I wouldn't have to worry about climbing stairs to get to our room or to the bathroom.

The day before we left for Ireland, Stephanie confirmed our arrangements to have a wheelchair waiting for us at the airport gate in Shannon. For some reason, though, it wasn't there when we arrived. Luckily, we'd bought a collapsible, three-legged combination cane-chair for me to use while sightseeing. It sure came in handy while waiting in line to go through Customs.

When Stephanie finally had an opportunity to ask a Customs agent where we could get a wheelchair, he nicely let us through Customs right away. Then we had another pleasant surprise: Our friends Arlene and Ron, who live in Wales, had come to meet us. We hadn't expected to see them until later in the day. They helped us get our luggage into our rental car and then guided Stephanie out of the airport as she got her bearings driving on the "wrong" side of the road to our first night's lodgings. After a short rest, we all met up again and went to a mock medieval dinner at a nearby castle.

We saw as much of the west coast of Ireland as we could. It was a great adventure. We saw beautiful scenery, met nice people and enjoyed the sheep grazing by the side of the road.

I felt like I had climbed a mountain when I struggled up a hill to see the remnants of an ancient fort. We had paid the farmer a pound (two dollars) for the privilege of making our way up the rocky slope on a narrow path of worn stone steps. I needed Stephanie's shoulder for balance. We spent a little extra time photographing the area, rereading the information in the tour book and enjoying the view. On our careful climb down, Stephanie said that the cows must enjoy this area too. I don't know how she managed to walk to the side of the path, giving me her shoulder for support and avoid the cow droppings.

We spent half a day on the grounds of the stately Mucross House, near Killarney. Tourists usually park their cars and then get a ride in a horse-drawn cart to the main house. But when we saw the cart, I shook my head. It was too high off the ground for me to get in. Stephanie tried to explain to the drivers, but they wouldn't take "no" for an answer. Instead, they hoisted me up onto the cart and away we went! It was too much fun for me to stay embarrassed.

One afternoon, we found a prehistoric burial site. It consisted of stones piled into a cone-shaped structure, with a small opening. To get to the site, we had to climb over a narrow gate that was designed to keep the cows and sheep out. I didn't have any trouble getting in but, on the way out, I got my weak right foot stuck and Stephanie had to yank it out.

That evening, when we went to dinner at a local pub, I had a lot of trouble walking from the car to the pub door. Although I didn't feel any pain, I could only shuffle the short distance to the restaurant. My right leg didn't seem to support me anymore. Stephanie asked what was wrong, but I didn't know. It wasn't until we returned to our bed-and-breakfast that I discovered the answer. When I took off my right shoe, I saw that the brace that was supposed to support my foot wasn't working. Stephanie must have broken the plastic hinge on it when she forced my foot out of the gate. Thankfully, she hadn't yanked any harder and broken my ankle!

The next morning, we asked our B&B hostess for directions to the nearest hospital. We assumed that every community had a small hospital with an orthopedic department. After all, people everywhere break arms and legs. Instead, we learned that the nearest prosthetics maker was in Cork, a two-hour drive away. As much as I had complained about things in the U.S., I suddenly realized how I'd been spoiled by the accessibility and availability of assistance for my disabilities back home.

Cork had not been on our itinerary, but this was a necessary detour. When we arrived that afternoon, we followed another patient, a frail, elderly woman, up a twisting, narrow flight of stairs to the prosthetics maker's cramped office.

Once we made our way into his workroom, he looked at my brace. "I learned to make these plastic braces in Boston just a few years ago," he said, "as part of a special exchange program sponsored by Boston-Irish families."

He clucked as he thought about how to solve my problem. "I can't repair the hinge, but I can melt on two stiff strips of plastic to keep the brace stable, in one position. That will provide support for your right foot. I really haven't seen this type of brace; with hinges, that is. It's very special."

"I asked his therapists to design it this way," Stephanie said. "I thought it would be easier for him going up or down steep slopes. They told me it wasn't a good idea. I guess they were right."

I didn't mind wearing an unhinged brace, so I told him to go ahead. "Thanks, thanks," I said, wishing I had more words to express my gratitude and relief. I decided that in the future, I'd take a spare brace when we traveled. When we got home, my physical therapists thought the Irishman had picked the right solution and done a nice job. They immediately cast me for another unhinged brace, the type I still use today.

On our way back to our B&B, we passed through some rain showers into the sunshine. Just outside a little town we saw the most beautiful rainbow, shimmering in all the colors of light, stretching in a soft, complete arch across the sky. Stephanie pulled to the side of the road and tried to photograph it. Maybe I would face greater challenges in future travels, but that day I felt like the world was mine again. *I felt that way myself!*

About six weeks after returning from Ireland, we decided it was time to begin looking for a more practical house. Going up and down the stairs was difficult and time-consuming, and it was impossible for me to take a cup of coffee up to the study. A friend referred us to a realtor who was very considerate and quickly learned what we were looking for: a rambler or ranch-style house, with the bedrooms, bathroom, living room and kitchen all on one level.

At that time it was a seller's market, and many of the houses in our price range were a little disappointing. We figured we'd look more seriously in the Spring, when more houses were likely to be on the market. But our plans changed a few weeks later, with the big stock market crash of 1987. We decided we'd better act immediately, before the mutual funds we wanted to use for the down payment evaporated.

Stephanie told the realtor that we wanted to find a house quickly and took some time off from work. The realtor previewed most of the houses, to rule out those with two-story climbs to the front door, steps without handrails, dark staircases down to the basement and other impediments. In one house, just as the realtor was noting that the description mentioned a soft spot in the porch floor, I stumbled over it. "I guess you found the soft spot!" she said as we all laughed.

Then we found the perfect place. It was a three-bedroom rambler on a quiet street, with a nice partly-finished basement, ideal for hobbies. I was pleased that I could understand the elements of the offer, and it sounded fair. We set our moving date for a few days before Christmas, so we could spend New Year's Eve in our new house.

A Year of Many Transitions
1988

Before we bought our house, we had asked Stephanie's father to inspect it. Joe was a commercial real estate appraiser, and since I worked for the city's real estate development department, we'd see each other on business occasionally. It was one of the many interests we had shared.

Joe came to visit us a number of times after we bought the house. A few months later he took ill. He was a heavy smoker and had been having trouble walking, then breathing. Then he developed a very bad cough. The doctors said he'd had a "silent" heart attack and now had congestive heart failure.

It was my turn to visit him in the hospital, then at his house. He wasn't a good patient. He was given strict instructions to go home and rest for weeks, which he didn't do. He slowed down a little, but not enough. A few weeks later, his heart gave out.

Stephanie was the first family member to get to the hospital, where she met her mother, brother and sister. She called me at my therapist's office to tell me. Then she took charge of the situation, drawing from that inner strength and sense of duty that had helped her survive my stroke, and keep our lives together. She called the funeral home, called the relatives, and calmed her mother.

Stephanie had inherited a lot of her positive attitude and energy from Joe. He had told me that I would make a full recovery, and was so convincing that I believed him. Stephanie tried to find solace in the fact that Joe died at his desk—he hadn't wanted to retire. That night, when she finally returned home, we cried together. This was an unexpected and devastating loss. Now this source of positive energy was gone, like the sun setting too fast.

The next day, I went with Stephanie and her family to meet with the Rabbi. I had so much I wanted to say about Joe, and was so frustrated that I couldn't speak. I wrote down what words I had, and asked Stephanie to help me, so I could ask the

Rabbi to express my feelings.

During the funeral, I sat with Stephanie's family, stunned at the feeling of loss. Joe was only sixty-five; he should have been around to share more of our lives. I had had a stroke and got better; he had survived his first heart attack, why couldn't he have survived that second one. It wasn't fair. I heard the Rabbi mention my name, and I knew he was reading from the notes I had given him.

I wish I could have given Joe more of a tribute. In my own way, I call on him every day. I use his image as a cue for recalling the letter "J": I swing my fist upward into a positive, powerful gesture. Joe was an inspiration, and I'll always remember him that way.

One of Joe's passions was airplanes, and he lost himself in building paper and balsa wood models of single-propeller planes. When Stephanie and I were first dating, she suggested I find a hobby, to pass the dreary winter weekends. After some research and soul-searching, I decided on model trains.

In my first house, I had built an elaborate HO scale model train layout in the basement. I had piled on as much as I could in the limited space. Stephanie complained that I had built into her "easement," the passageway to get from the stairs to the washer and dryer. And carrying the clothes basket, she often scraped her arm on my control panel.

The structure was so well built, and anchored into the walls, that I couldn't take it with me when we moved to our new house. Plus, one of the features of the new house was its large, partially finished basement, perfect for a new layout. Even so, it hurt deep inside when we had to hire a handyman to sledge-hammer the old layout into pieces so he could take it away. He also sledge-hammered the wheel chair ramp off the front door, which made me feel better.

After we moved, I went to a meeting of the local model train club, which I had joined when I first started working on my model. I was looking for ideas for my new layout. A few days later, Chip, one of the club members called and offered, without me asking, to come over with Brian, a friend of his, and help me build the table and put together the basic tracks to get me started.

I was touched and excited. I really felt special, and thankful that these men were going to help me. Since I hadn't regained any strength in my right hand, I couldn't do the construction work needed to build a sturdy table.

That Saturday, Chip and Brian arrived early, with books and plans, and measured the space. They tried to negotiate with Stephanie to take over more of the lower level, but she refused.

After some consideration, Chip showed me a diagram of a simple layout in one of his books. "What do you think of this one, Paul," he asked.

"No," I said. I didn't have the words to explain why I didn't like it. I pointed to the parts I liked and said, "good," and the parts I didn't like and said, "no."

"You can't build it like that," Brian said. "You need this much turning radius, and room for an inside line."

We finally agreed on a plan for a table fourteen feet long and five feet at the widest part, which was too deep for me to reach across, but they said it wouldn't work any other way. I would have to find a way to climb on a step stool, balance and reach over. Chip sketched the layout, and made calculations for the lumber and hardware.

Off we went to a building supply store. For me, it was like running a marathon to keep up with them. I appreciated their kindness in volunteering to help me, but they weren't sensitive to my limitations. They walked too quickly through the store for me with my cane and half a dead body to lug around, but they didn't seem to notice that I was struggling behind. I worked hard to hold in my growing frustration and anger. Getting my table built was the goal, and I needed to keep myself focused on that goal. Instead of worrying about what they were doing, I decided to wait for them near the check-out counter.

Chip and Brian returned three or four more weekends to finish the table. Once, when I was trying to help, Chip told me that I was in the way. I just had to swallow my pride.

When the table was completed, I could start to work on my plans. I was modeling the Northwest U.S. for a freight railroad. At one end, I planned to build a mountain and a river, and at the other end, a seaport, complete with train yards, factories, warehouses, and other industrial buildings.

One of the rewards of a hobby is the creative process itself. I built my models from plastic kits, following the instructions, and visualizing my goal: getting the model to look like the picture on the box. A few times a week, I would work on it for an hour or so, moving a step closer to achieving my goal and creating something of my own. It took me away from my everyday problems, into a different world—into "Paulville"—the world I was creating from mountain to seaport. Here, I was king. Here, my decisions were final. Here, what I said was the law. Here, I was in control (now that my friends from the club had completed their work).

Even before my stroke, I took great care to put the pieces together and paint them to look as realistic as possible. After my stroke, I had to do everything with one hand. I needed to find a way to hold the model pieces while I applied glue or pushed the pieces together. I found the answer in a modeler's tool catalog. They had miniature tools for model trains, doll house construction, and other hobbies and crafts requiring fine tools and instruments. From the catalog I ordered a set of tiny clamps; a set of small, heavy weights; a metal tray with turned-up edges and half a dozen small magnets.

To see the smallest features of my models without using a hand-held magnifier, I ordered goggles with magnifying lens from the catalog. Other items I borrowed from around the house, like a lamp with a long arm that clamped onto my work table, tweezers, an under-the-counter bottle opener, a small plastic cart with basket drawers and wheels I could pull around, and toothpicks. After I had knocked over the glue bottle about ten times and Stephanie complained about the smell and worried about me damaging what was left of my brain by sniffing the fumes, she rigged a holder for my glue bottle by cutting a hole in a small paper plate.

It took a lot longer to build each model, but since I was so lost in each project, the time didn't matter. And it felt so good when I finished one. A few years later, I was particularly proud of a signal tower I had completed. I entered it into my model train club's annual convention and competition—and I won third place! I was so proud, I felt like my old self again. I had the award framed and it's still hanging on the wall in my den.

Another favorite memory of mine with the model train club was the day we went on a tour of the Amtrak maintenance yard. I had to buy a hard hat to go on the tour. I managed well, although I needed to take someone's arm to climb over the tracks and negotiate some parts of the yard. I was amazed to see the big trains and maintenance equipment life-sized and up close. It helped me to picture what other structures I might want for my model rail yard.

The tour guide spoke too fast for me to get all of his explanation, but it didn't matter. I was so happy to see and smell and touch and be part of this. One of the club members took pictures, and gave me a snapshot of me in my hard hat, with two other men, looking up in awe at one of the trains. Seeing that picture made me feel like a real man.

To show my appreciation for all the club meant to me, I volunteered to work on the annual regional meeting, hosted by my club at a hotel not too far from where I lived. Stephanie explained to the chairman what tasks I could handle. He decided to give me the job of registrar. All the registration forms would come to me, and I would type names, addresses, phone numbers and the sessions they had signed up for into a database he developed in Lotus, and installed on my home computer. He showed me how to enter the forms, wrote out instructions, then watched me do it.

"Paul, this is going to take you forever," he said. "Are you sure you want to do it?"

"Yes, yes," I answered. This was very important to me.

"Work...type. Work. Lotus, type, work," I said, trying to explain that I did similar data entry using a Lotus spreadsheet at work. After a few guesses, he understood me. Actually, as slow as I seemed to him, I was typing much faster than when I started back to work.

Twice a week, I'd receive packets of registration forms in the mail from the treasurer. I disciplined myself to spend at least an hour every evening after dinner to enter the information. It was hard for me, but it made me feel like a full member of the club, a teammate pulling his weight.

During the awards dinner, they surprised me with a small plaque in recognition of my work. They were so impressed with my attitude and interest in helping. I loved walking up to the podium, hearing the applause, and feeling the support from all of these special friends.

A few years later, at a point where my layout was overflowing with models, and I was trying to persuade Stephanie to let me expand, one of my cats tested it. He jumped off a shelf onto the mountain, thinking it was a solid mountain, and not a paper-mache over chicken-wire fake. It crumbled under his weight, and when I found it, my beautiful mountain with all the realistic rocks and scrub brush was mashed in, flat as a pizza. I called one of the club members over for a consultation (and consolation). He suggested removing the remains of the mountain, instead of rebuilding it, to give me room to expand my city and port structures.

Stephanie had wanted a cat for many years. But our house in Arlington seemed too small and we couldn't agree on where to put the litter box. Once we moved to our new house she asked again. She had always had pets growing up. I did not—unless you count having a chick until it was big enough to give to a nearby farmer. I wasn't allergic to animals, but I'd never lived with one and didn't know what to expect. I wanted to learn more, ask questions, analyze my options.

One Saturday in early summer, Stephanie convinced me to go to a "cat" day at a local library sponsored by the Humane

Society. They had dozens of cats, all ages, sizes, colors, shapes, and breeds. They explained to us that we should adopt two kittens, so they would keep each other company during the day when we weren't home. They even gave a discount in the "adoption" fee for two. There were two older kittens, about twelve weeks old: a friendly outgoing one, and a shy one. I was immediately attracted to the friendly one, and held him for a while. He was soft and lovable.

I usually don't do things on the spur of the moment, but Stephanie didn't want to leave without the cats, and I reluctantly agreed. We signed the "adoption" papers, paid the contribution to the Humane Society, and agreed to have the cats neutered when they turned six months old. We put them in a cardboard pet carrier and took them home.

Stephanie carried them down to the basement, where she placed their litter box. Then she left me in charge, while she ran out to the store to get cat food and supplies. The minute she left, both kittens ran up the stairs and into the living room. They moved so fast, I couldn't keep track of them. Suddenly, the shy, gray kitten, Mack, ran up the curtains and dangled near the ceiling. I couldn't reach him, but I yelled and shook the curtains to try to get him down. He finally let go and fell to the carpeted floor, then ran off. Meanwhile, his friendly blond-colored brother, Sam, ran up the back of the sofa and clung to it with his little claws. I managed to get him off, then pushed the sofa against the wall.

I was exhausted trying to watch them as they ran through the house. And I got angry. I wasn't ready for this kind of behavior. My stroke made me too slow. When Stephanie came home, I exploded. Over the next few weeks, I continued to be angry about the situation. Stephanie seemed to spend all her free time playing with the kittens. I enjoyed watching them wrestle and play together, and Sam always came to me to be petted, but I just couldn't relate to them.

My chief job in caring for them was cleaning their litter box. I won this job because my physical therapists had advised me to go up and down the stairs at least once a day to stretch my leg muscles. In our old house in Arlington, I had climbed the stairs many times a day, since the bathroom, study and bedroom were on the second floor. In our new rambler, bought for the very purpose of avoiding stairs, I only went down to the basement a few times a week to work on my model trains.

Then, Stephanie went out of town for a four-day business meeting, leaving me all alone to care for the kittens. Usually, when Stephanie traveled, I felt really lonely. But this time, I didn't. The kittens greeted me when I came in the front door, and followed me around all evening. They jumped on my desk, on the bed, went everywhere I went. I talked to them. They didn't seem to mind my aphasic speech. They gave me a warm feeling inside that I had never felt before. When Stephanie came back from her trip, she noticed the difference right away.

The kittens helped me with another breakthrough. I had been struggling in speech therapy with my writing. After much intense work, I was able to put together most of a sentence. Now, it was time to try building a paragraph, a complex task for me. Before my stroke, I had taken this for granted. I had always been able to write clearly. This was all lost when I had the stroke. It knocked out the language center in my brain, so other brain cells had to take over the routine of pulling out words, and the nearly impossible job of understanding the irrational structure of English grammar.

My first assignment was to write a paragraph about the kittens. Somehow, they inspired me in a special way, and suddenly, writing a paragraph about them came easily. I had jumped up to the next plateau, just like Mack jumping up the curtains.

A few months later, I made a breakthrough in reading. I had bought a book on "edge cities," the suburban centers of commerce, like Tysons Corners, near me. I remember sitting in bed with the book, Sam sleeping on my leg. I couldn't read a whole chapter in one sitting, but I could read a paragraph, understand it, and go onto the next paragraph. I felt wonderful, like my old self. I was overcoming the aphasia: moving from understanding single words, to whole sentences to whole paragraphs. The progress was slow, but I was continuing to make progress more

2½ yo. after the stroke

than two and a half years after my stroke. It gave me great hope *Not 50%?!* that I would slowly but surely regain all of my old abilities. It gave me the motivation to work on.

I also saw gains in the realignment of my torso, hip, leg and foot. I wouldn't have noticed these except that my plastic leg-foot brace started to rub and hurt. My physical therapists cast me for a new brace, this one yet another step closer to a more normal form. After I got used to it, I realized that I was taking fewer and fewer pain pills. I went from taking two pills every four hours when I first came home from the hospital, to taking them once a day or less—if I had walked a little too much or stood a little too long. Now, I needed them less than once a week.

My therapists also noticed that the pain in my paralyzed right arm and hand was gone. At first, they couldn't touch it without my grimacing. Now, I could complete a half hour of therapy exercises before I noticed any discomfort.

They suggested I try my luck at swimming again. When I had tried it that first summer home from the hospital, my right arm floated up away from my body in the water, a position that was too painful for me to continue. This time there was almost no pain at all.

I was really excited to get back into the water. I had been concerned that despite all the physical therapy, I was not getting much cardiovascular exercise. Before my stroke, I enjoyed swimming. Learning to swim laps had been a special test for my courage when I was a teenager, overcoming my fear of putting my face in the water. It had made me feel like a man to conquer that fear. In the last three years, I had challenges that took so much more courage to conquer, that returning to the swimming pool was like going to a friend's home.

The pool's staff found a volunteer who helped me readjust to one-handed, one-legged swimming. He put a floatation vest on me, so I could concentrate on my stroke—that is swimming stroke, not brain stroke. I relearned a breast stroke and a back stroke. To my surprise, the back stroke was easier and I found myself doing it for most of my workout.

The only problem was that I was scraping the toes of my weak right foot on the bottom or side of the pool. My therapists suggested wearing pool slippers, but I couldn't find any. I had to settle for buying a pair of canvas slippers with rubber soles. To keep them from falling off in the water, Stephanie sewed on Velcro straps. They were ladies' slippers, but at least they were gray, and after the initial shudder, my manhood was able to get past it. I had to focus on my goal: a safe swim.

I only needed four lessons to regain my confidence in the water. Stephanie insisted that I always wear the floatation vest so I wouldn't have to worry if I became too tired in the water. I didn't mind, it made it easier to do laps. The most frustrating part was how much time it took me to change in the locker room. Unlike my pre-stroke days, when I could jump into the shower, dress and be out in a few minutes, it took me half an hour to change into my swimsuit, and almost an hour afterwards to shower and put on my street clothes. But I didn't let it get in my way, and that summer I went to the pool at least once a week, building up to forty-five minutes of swimming laps. It made me feel both energized and relaxed, and was an important step in my recovery.

I was moving forward, slowly but surely reclaiming my old self. Then I had a miserable setback. When I had returned to the D.C. government almost two years earlier, I thought that I would regain my speech in a few months, and soon after be able to take on more of my old responsibilities. My boss had been tolerant, but I wasn't making progress fast enough. The department was under some pressure, and my protector, the head of the department, was planning to leave.

My boss called me and Stephanie to a meeting. My direct supervisor was there, and someone from the personnel office.

"Paul, you are the most courageous person I have ever known," my boss said. I smiled, feeling that maybe the distance that had grown between us was healing.

"You know that the department is being reorganized, and we're scheduled to move in six months," he continued. "In

118

planning our new space, we had to make some decisions." He stopped, looking for words. "The staff is really stretched trying to handle all the projects on our plate. We really miss how much you carried by yourself before...before... I appreciate the tasks you're doing now, but it's not the same level of work. I asked if I could add another project specialist position, but the budget office turned me down. So, I need your 'slot.'" He stopped to let me catch the meaning of his words.

My "slot," my job position and pay level, the "slot" I was occupying part time. I was just a "slot" to him. I felt the Grand Canyon had opened between us.

He continued. "The personnel office has looked high and low for another position in our department. But we just can't find one. There isn't much turnover, and when someone leaves, the budget people usually cut the slot. You've been a good employee, and I'm sure that you'll find a job in one of the other city departments."

I felt betrayed. He had been my friend. Before my stroke, I had carried a dozen projects for the department, including some of the most important and sensitive ones. And I had seen them completed with great success. Buildings were built, stores and hotels opened because of my liaison work. I had made him look good. He had counted on me as a confidant, and I thought we had a special relationship.

After my stroke, his attitude had changed completely. He didn't want to spend time with me, he almost never talked to me. It had hurt my feelings to lose his confidence and friend- ship. Then he cut out my heart, destroyed my self-respect when he told me he didn't want me in his department any more.

If he had really wanted to stand up for me, I believed that he could have kept me. There were other employees who were much less productive than me, even after my stroke, who clocked in every day. But he didn't want me. This rejection was almost as hard to bear as all my disabilities. I wasn't prepared for it. I had assumed that I would continue to work here part time, as I continued my rehabilitation, then return full time for a few years.

Eventually, I thought, I would leave the government for a private-sector job, as I had been planning to do just before my stroke. I had assumed that I would be able to control my timetable. My boss' decision robbed my of that control, and threw my plans into chaos. And I didn't have a lot of emotional padding to absorb the shock.

Stephanie and I discussed my options. I didn't want to look for work in another city department. I had no interest in health, or welfare or other programs. So, I decided to retire on disability. Fortunately, the government's disability program allowed me to draw a pension, work up to a certain level, and most importantly, hold onto my health insurance. I'd continue with my speech, physical and occupational therapy, and look for a part-time job.

My retirement paperwork was "rushed" through the bureaucracy, so it only took six months to complete. On my last day, they held a retirement party for me. It was a bitter- sweet moment. I enjoyed the attention, the good food, taking photos, and all the kind words. But I hated that I had been forced to leave, forced to this point against my wishes. I wanted to stay and work, not retire.

About two months before my final day at the city job, Stephanie and I returned to the Department of Rehabilitative Services, to re-open my file. After reviewing my papers, the intake counselor looked me in the eye and said, "You'll be getting a good pension. Why do you want to work?"

I was stunned. I tried to tell him, with Stephanie's help in "translating," that I was only thirty-eight. I was a young man, I didn't want to retire. I wanted to work. I wanted to earn money to show my worth. I was motivated and had a supportive wife and family. I would be his best client. Why was he asking me such a demoralizing question!

He also suggested that I try to find work somewhere else in the city government first, instead of retiring. He didn't think I had much of a chance of finding any work. I wanted to strangle him; I wanted to report him to his superiors. But what good would it do me? I needed DRS's assistance, so I had to swallow hard and play along. I hated being so dependent, and as the job search progressed, I realized that my success would come from using what parts of the system I could to my advantage, while doing much of the work myself, with Stephanie's help.

The intake counselor had us sign some papers. The next step would be another evaluation of my work potential. I dreaded that process, since the tests seemed to have so little to do with real work.

Again, the evaluation came back concluding that I wasn't qualified for competitive employment. It didn't mention that I had actually accomplished significant clerical and computer work in my government job. I was so angry. This was a repeat of my experience two years earlier. I showed the report to my speech therapist, who again agreed that it didn't portray an accurate assessment of my abilities. But, the evaluator stuck by her tests.

Because of my persistence, DRS referred me to a "work hardening" program that had been established for people with mental disabilities. The counselor insisted that the staff in this program understood the difference between the disabilities associated with a stroke—in my case, language problems, and only being able to use one hand—and those associated with other mental health conditions. I didn't think that after working for so many years, including two years after my stroke, I needed "work hardening." That's the jargon to describe training a person to come to work on time, stay focused on a project, and interact in socially acceptable ways. I didn't need that; I had proven I could do all that in the last two years. But to have a job placement counselor help me find a job, I had to do it their way.

At the same time, I enrolled in a group that met two mornings a week, sponsored by the Multiple Sclerosis Society. It was designed to help people who had worked for some years, then became disabled in adulthood. It was a perfect program for me. It consisted of three phases: the first was learning to take charge of your life and building up self-esteem and self-management skills. These sessions helped me and the ten other participants to deal with the changes we were facing in our lives, and to understand some of the adjustments we needed to make in how we saw ourselves.

ᐧ It helped me to count on the job skills I still had, and put aside the professional skills I'd lost. Even though I completed all the assignments, I didn't accept that I might be losing my professional life. Instead, I convinced myself that this was a temporary disability, a temporary change in job status, until I could finish my therapy and return to my old self.

Phase two and three of the MS program involved job seeking techniques and then going out and looking for work. One assignment was creating a video resume. I dressed up in my best navy blue interview suit, white shirt and conservative tie. Since I couldn't say more than a few words, one of the male counselors read my work objective and related skills as a narrator, while I smiled into the camera.

Stephanie came to watch, which might have been a mistake. I didn't realize how hard it was to smile naturally for three minutes while someone talked about you. We looked at the first take. They wanted me to nod a little, to acknowledge what the voice was saying. So I forced a smile and nodded. Stephanie started to laugh, and ruined the take. She said I looked like one of those toys with a bobbing head people put in the back of their cars. She had a point—we all laughed, then had an easier time shooting the final take.

Meanwhile, the DRS job counselor had arranged some job interviews for me. I told her that I wanted a part-time position, ten to fifteen hours a week, in banking, finance, or real estate development, using my clerical skills. The interviews were disasters. In one, while I was leaning on a handrail to climb a flight of stairs to reach the office, the handrail came off in my hand and I almost fell down the stairs. In another, the counselor who came with me made me sound like a charity case, and didn't give me a chance to say anything about myself. I came back to the MS group and shared my unhappy experiences. It really helped having their support.

By early November, I had finished the MS program, but I still didn't have a job. My job counselor said that private employers needed part-time workers for five days a week, mornings or afternoons. But I didn't want to compromise my intense speech and physical therapy schedule, since they were my ticket back to professional work.

So, we decided to go to plan B: looking for a volunteer job that might eventually grow into a paying position. Stephanie and I went to the library to find names of local associations related to my areas of professional interest. We copied over a hundred names, addresses and phone numbers of potential associations, and gave the list to my counselor. She called and called and called. Finally, a financial association agreed to a temporary, part time job. They couldn't give me a salary, but were able to give me a small stipend to defray my commuting costs. I started just before Christmas.

Fortunately, their office was downtown, just two blocks from Stephanie's office, so I could drive in with her on the two days I worked. I worked in the personnel office on Tuesdays, completing "mail merge" form letters for job applicants, entering health insurance data and other benefit information, general filing, copying and office work. It was boring, but I was learning some new things, keeping up my computer and office skills, and meeting new people.

On Fridays, I worked in the association's budget office for their financial manager. He was really nice, and gave me some interesting work tracking the association's revenues and expenses for the training programs they offered to their membership, monthly budgeting and planning, experience with cash flow projections, and other helpful accounting and financial management experience.

By that New Year's Eve, three years after my ruptured aneurysm, I had weathered a year of emotional ups and downs. I was working harder than ever on my "real" job: physical and speech therapy. I had a new routine and the hope that maybe by this time next year, I would be a regular, paid employee of the association.

Always Open With a Joke
1989-1990

From time-to-time, my DRS job counselor would call to check on my progress. I was trying my best to prove that I was a valuable employee to the association. But timing is everything, and unfortunately, this was a time when the financial industry was not doing well. The association's members were going out of business or merging with others, and I could tell from the plans being developed by my boss, that the association's leaders were doing all they could to prevent laying off staff.

A few months later, in the early summer, when I had been hoping to find a permanent, paying job with them, they cut my volunteer hours back to one day a week. Having a whole day with little to do gave me too much time to think about myself. I started to feel depressed and hopeless. My speech and physical therapists and Stephanie repeated that I was continuing to make progress on all fronts. But it was so very, very slow. I felt like I was going around in circles, and never going to get back to my old self.

Up till now, I just hadn't had time to feel sorry for myself. My schedule was too full and at the end of the day, I was too tired to worry. I didn't realize how important having a job was. I needed to feel that someone was willing to pay my wages. Luckily, between my disability pension and Stephanie's salary, I didn't have to work in order to eat, but I felt that I had to work in order to live.

Stephanie became alarmed at my dark moods, and looked around for ways to fill my time. In addition to a list of errands—laundry, shopping, post office, bill paying—she suggested that I think about volunteering some time to the county political party. So, one Tuesday morning I went up to the party's headquarters to help. I couldn't make phone calls, so I looked up phone numbers. But my handwriting was too large and sloppy for their records, since I was a right-handed person still learning how to write with my left hand.

Instead, they found me a position in the tiny campaign office of my state delegate, who was running for re-election that summer. My job was to file her "walking" cards, three-by-five-inch cards with names, addresses, and key political information about voters. She carried these cards as she walked through the neighborhoods in her district, making notes on the questions raised by the people she met. When she returned to her office, the cards were all mixed up, and usually thrown onto a pile. I sorted and filed them by street number. My delegate and her campaign manager—who was her only staff person—enjoyed what they were doing, enjoyed life, and shared their positive attitude with me. I always left the office feeling cheery. And I felt that they would always be my friends, which proved true, even as my delegate succeeded a few years later in becoming elected to Congress.

At the end of the summer, I turned forty. Forty is a significant turning point in most people's lives, regardless of their experiences, accomplishments, lifestyle, ambitions, or health. My parents decided to give me a big party to celebrate it. I think they were celebrating the fact that I lived to see it. They invited all of my Philadelphia friends, and Gary, who drove up from Washington to join us. To my surprise, my brother came in from the West Coast with his new wife.

I really enjoyed being surrounded by my friends and their positive energy. During the party, I gave my very first speech, and although it was short and simple, I was very nervous giving it. But I needed to thank everyone for their continued support and encouragement, and to let them know how much I appreciated their friendship. They were true to me in my time of need.

I was also happy to spend time with my brother. He was a vocational counselor and we talked a lot about my job hunting and my disappointment that volunteering for the financial association hadn't turned into a permanent position.

"Paul, why don't you take another approach," my brother

said. "Maybe the employers are bothered by you showing up with your job counselor for interviews. Maybe they think you can't do anything by yourself."

Since my phone skills weren't very good, I needed my counselor to set up the appointment. But my brother suggested that I go to the interview alone. "Do you really need someone to be there with you," he asked. "Look how good your non-verbal communication skills are. I understand what you mean with your gestures and notepad."

He was pumping me up, and giving me something new to think about. He also suggested that seeing a disabled person might make an employer uncomfortable. So it was up to me to put them at ease. I'd never thought of that. I'd just assumed that everyone would accept me for who I was, and not be bothered by my disabilities. I also never thought that I had the power to actually put someone else at ease; that maybe this was my responsibility.

This was a breakthrough for me. For the first time, I saw myself from the outside. And I saw how I could take control. After the party, after this talk with my brother, after this breakthrough, I came back to Washington and felt like I could conquer the world!

Stephanie helped me go through the newspaper help-wanted ads. She found an ad for a part time accounting clerk for a real estate management company. This sounded like a dream job for me. It was both real estate and finance, with a company that had a good reputation. The ad said to show up for an interview between nine a.m. and noon on Wednesday. So I did. And I went alone. I was going to try my brother's approach.

I needed an opening "joke" to put the interviewer at ease. This seemed impossible. My speech wasn't good enough to tell a joke so that a stranger would understand what I meant. Stephanie came to the rescue. She read the comics everyday, and found a comic strip where the character decided to go into business doing odd jobs. The character pestered her friend, offering to do chores around the house, or any odd job he wanted. After too much pestering, he got frustrated with her and told her to "take a hike." Her response was, "Odd request, but a job's a job."

I thought this really captured my spirit. I was willing to do any job. I was a hard worker, and not above doing clerical work, even though I had once been a professional. Right now, I just wanted to work and be valued. I wanted a paycheck and a chance to show how much I could do.

I put on my best interview suit and tie, and took the subway down to the interview. I presented myself to the receptionist, showed her the help-wanted ad I had clipped out of the newspaper, and waited for my turn. The purchasing manager who had placed the ad escorted me to his office.

I gave him a copy of the comic strip, and gestured to show that this was just like me. He read it and laughed. It worked! I showed him my resume, and the three letters of recommendation that I was given when I left the city government. He asked me a few questions and was very nice to me. When I left his office, I felt great. My brother was right. I could do it by myself.

The next day, the purchasing manager called. I got the job! That was one of the happiest days of my life. My first day would be the next Monday, the first of October. I was starting over and it felt great.

My primary task in my new job was filing invoices. I had my own desk and worked with two other people in the purchasing office. I had to overcome some unexpected problems. With just one hand, it was hard to open the folder in the file drawer and neatly drop the paper in the right place. I asked my occupational therapist for help. She suggested using large plastic hair clips to hold open the folders, or a weight I had used to hold books open. The weight worked okay, but some times it would drop down between the folders and I'd have trouble getting it out.

The job was boring, but I felt that it was a good start. I believed that I could work my way up in this type of company. And it was in my chosen career field, real estate. I worked three mornings a week downtown, and continued my speech and

127

physical therapy.

When New Years Eve came, I had been employed for three months and felt happy and hopeful. Stephanie and I made plans to visit my parents at their winter apartment in Florida over the President's Day holiday in February. And I was starting to think about future travel plans and other goals.

4 months

About three weeks later, I noticed that the other two staffers were meeting in my boss' office with the door closed. It upset me. I didn't understand why they were shutting me out. *I only worked part time, why didn't they have these meetings when I wasn't there. What were they talking about?* When I asked, they told me it was "nothing." I guess my intuition was telling me it was "something." And I was right. A few days later, my boss called me into his office. He told me that he needed a full time person for my job, and so had to let me go. That very day. No notice, just "goodbye."

My boss said that he thought by letting me go immediately, I could extend my trip to Florida. But that was the last thing I wanted to do. I was crushed. I couldn't believe it. I was feeling angry and sad and so many other emotions. What was I going to do? First I was asked to leave my city job, now this. I hated the new pattern of my life: the ups and downs of having a job, then losing it. It was a terrible torture on top of my stroke.

I felt like I was half a person, trying to drag half a dead body everywhere I went. I felt like giant marbles were stuck in my mouth, always in the way when I wanted to say something. And now I felt burdened by the shame of being fired—twice. How was one man going to carry all of this. How was I supposed to carry on?

I talked to Stephanie, and she helped me as always, by focusing on the next step. Look ahead, don't look back, she had said. I called the DRS job counselor who had found me the volunteer job at the financial association. She said that I had to get DRS to reopen my file, then refer me to her. This would take a few weeks. Meanwhile, I went through the newspaper looking for work, and mailing out my resume, using a form letter

128

Stephanie had written for me, then sending copies of the cover letters and ads to my job counselor.

Calling and calling DRS was the only way to get an appointment. I felt desperate, I sounded desperate. I was very motivated to get a new job. A different DRS intake counselor met with me for over two hours, but the results were the same. She insulted me and concluded that I was unemployable.

She asked me to show her how much I could move my paralyzed right arm. How much could I lift, what medications was I taking, what did my doctor say, what happened to me in the hospital, why was I still taking physical and speech therapy, who was paying, how could I possibly work? These were the stupid questions she asked me. I was looking for a clerical job, and I had already worked for two years in the city government; for almost a year as a volunteer; and for four months at a paying job I'd found myself. *Just refer me to my job counselor so I can find another job!* The only smart thing she did was to sign the referral paperwork.

Thankfully, the job placement counselor had started right away to follow up on the ads I had responded to. She explained why someone with a list of professional jobs on his resume wanted a low-level clerical position. The day before I left for my long weekend in Florida, she got me an interview with the accounting supervisor at a nonprofit group. That news, and the sun in Florida, helped my attitude a lot. When I came home, I was charged up.

Again, I went on the interview by myself, armed with my comic strip opener. A few days later, the supervisor called my job counselor to tell her he would hire me. I started the following week, commuting downtown just three subway stops further than my job with the real estate company. My position was part time, four hours in the morning Monday through Thursday (so I could continue my therapy in the afternoons) and most of the day, Friday. I was doing bookkeeping, tracking daily receipts, invoices, filing, entering data, using the computer, copying, and checking to make sure the numbers were entered correctly. At the end of the month, I helped with monthly billings and reconciliations.

My new boss scared me a few times; he had a terrible temper. He was a bear for time-keeping. If he saw me heading to the men's room with a magazine, he'd yell at me. When I came back from lunch on Fridays, he would scold me for taking more than half an hour.

Some of my coworkers accepted me; but the two clerks with whom I shared an office ignored me. They would carry on conversations as if I wasn't there. If I said anything to them, they wouldn't answer. I really felt like an ant working there.

Stephanie was so concerned about my reaction to the situation that she suggested I look for a new job. But I'm not a quitter, and I wasn't going to quit this job because some of the people were mean to me. Eventually, the supervisor who hired me left, and a much nicer man replaced him. The clerks also left and were replaced with some people who were a little more friendly.

Even though the work was boring, I was learning new things, and settling into a comfortable routine. I woke up early, did my stretching exercises, showered, dressed in a suit and tie, commuted into town, worked for four hours, then came back, had lunch, and drove to my speech or physical therapy appointment. After that, three afternoons a week, my tutor came and drilled me on words and sentences. After dinner, I worked on speech homework for an hour or so, watched television, then went to bed. It was an exhausting schedule, but having a busy routine that was punctuated with paychecks kept me happy and gave me little time to worry about myself.

Once in a while I would have a really good day. I would complete a new task in physical therapy and Sally would congratulate me and change my home exercises to the next level. Or a friend who I hadn't seen in a few weeks would tell me it was a little easier to talk to me. These small victories kept me motivated.

Other times, I'd get frustrated with the never-ending speech homework, and ask Jenny to put a time and date on when I'd be back to normal. She was always honest with me, and treated me with great respect. So when she told me that I was making a lot of progress, but she didn't think I would get back to my previous professional level, it would send me into a deep funk. Stephanie would spend the evening trying to cheer me up. She told me it was my choice to stay with therapy—I could quit anytime. But I didn't want to stop, so after a good night's sleep, I'd continue with my routine.

Most therapy days, I went to the same fast food restaurant for lunch. I got to know the counter staff and always greeted them warmly. If I missed a few days, maybe to have lunch somewhere else with friends, they'd ask where I'd been. These little moments made me feel special, and helped me overcome the embarrassing times, like when I had trouble carrying my tray with one hand and my cup of soda fell over, getting soda on me and all over the floor.

It was never easy living with my disabilities, and with the memories of how I was before the stroke. The ups and downs were higher and lower than before, and I learned to appreciate the good things, and focus on my goals. Sometimes, despite my motivation and can-do attitude, strangers forced me to feel that I was different.

To commute to my job at the nonprofit group, I drove to the subway station, and parked in a parking space for handicapped drivers. I carried my newspaper, homework and other things in a soft leather briefcase with a shoulder strap. Once in the station, I sometimes had a little problem fitting through the turnstile. I was still a little clumsy in my walking, and the bulky briefcase threw me off. I needed my good left hand to insert the farecard, and had to reach across, since the ticket slots were all on the right side.

If I heard a train coming, I tried to rush up the escalator to catch it. But I was really slow, and had to hold onto the left hand rail. Sometimes other commuters pushed me trying to get to the train. Because I didn't carry a cane, and wasn't in a wheelchair, they didn't notice that I was disabled.

Getting on the train was difficult with the other commuters hurrying on, and once inside, as the doors closed and the train

131

started to move, I usually stumbled and lost my balance before I could get seated. Sometimes I'd have to ask a stranger to give up his seat in the designated handicapped seating. Too many times, they'd ignore me, refuse to move, or look at me like I was crazy. I didn't like having to ask for a seat. I didn't like having to tell total strangers that I was disabled. I didn't like being too unsteady to stand. My right leg and foot were still too weak to support me for more than a few minutes, and the subway ride in the mornings was almost thirty minutes.

Most people read on the subway, and I was no exception. I liked to read the newspaper. Opening and folding a newspaper when you are jammed into a tight seat on a packed subway car can be tricky for a normal person. For me with one hand, it required a little creativity. I had to pull it out of my briefcase without emptying the entire contents, and fold it in fourths, then bend down the corner of the page, all while trying to keep it and my briefcase from slipping off my lap.

Leaving the train at my stop was another challenge. I had to think about each of my movements as if I was working the controls of a machine. First I had to be sure that both feet were firmly flat on the floor. I had some trouble lifting myself from a sitting position unless I had a pole to grab. Sometimes this would be difficult if I was sitting on the right side of the seat and could not easily reach the pole with my left hand. Once I was standing, I had to plant my feet so I felt secure enough to deal with the pressure of the other commuters trying to exit the train, and the momentum of the train as it usually jerked to a stop. Then I had to let go of the pole and walk off without stumbling.

Once in a while, I'd lose my temper. If someone pushed me, I'd push back as hard as I could, to show that I "counted." But the others were usually too much in a hurry or self-absorbed to notice or care. Looking back at myself before my stroke, I think that I was probably like some of these strangers. I wondered how many disabled people I had pushed out of the way without realizing it.

Macho...Macho...Man...

1991-1992

Now that I was settled into a comfortable routine with the nonprofit group, I could start to set other goals.

I had read about a university lab that was studying speech and language disorders and decided that I wanted to join their study. I wanted to help myself and others. By being in touch with the experts, I thought that I might eventually meet a scientist who could "cure" me.

Stephanie called the university's "cognitive neuropsychology" lab and convinced the researchers to interview me. I was a little nervous. I wanted to pass all their tests. I wanted them to include me in their study.

The researchers were very nice, and most of the tests were reading or writing words, pointing to "yes" or "no," listening to sentences, repeating what I heard, defining words. Stephanie and I learned a lot about my aphasia, and how my language "machine" was reset by the stroke. I could pick the right definitions for college-level words, but had a terrible time with "push" and "pull." The researchers explained that paired opposites, like push and pull, yes and no, give and take, were so close in meaning—or where they were stored in the brain—that it was common among stroke patients to confuse them.

I also had trouble understanding sentences where the grammar was a little mixed up. I could hear or read the words, "the girl smelled the flower" and "the flower smelled the girl" and understand the concept, but I couldn't pick which sentence was right.

One session with the researchers proved that I'd be a good subject for their study. I had the energy and mental focus to work for a whole day with only a lunch break. I saw these sessions, held on a Saturday every six or eight weeks, as a challenge to outlast the researchers. And usually I won. I could tire out two researchers in a row. I came away from those days exhausted and energized by the sense of my victory.

I know that targeted speech therapy is more effective in helping a person to regain language skills, but these intense testing sessions were very stimulating, helping me pull out new words, new phrases, new meanings. I felt myself making progress. Over the many years that I participated, I continued to make measurable progress in my speech, which the researchers noticed as well. My "cure" wasn't found, but I gained a lot from the experience, and someday, I hope, the research will help others.

Finally, our budget had recovered from buying a new house and my changing jobs three times. I was ready to plan another trip overseas. We went to the travel agent and brought home a pile of brochures. Spain looked very inviting. Stephanie decided that she didn't want to drive in Spain, since she didn't understand enough Spanish to read the road signs. We found a ten-day bus tour that looked fun. There were trade-offs between traveling on your own and taking a bus tour, but I became more excited as I read about Spain.

To get into shape for all the walking I'd do on the tour, I tried to walk every day. By the time we took our trip in late September, I could walk more than a mile. The first two days in Madrid, we were on our own to explore the city. Our hotel was in the downtown area. We made our way around the city, walking a few blocks until my leg got tired, stopping in a restaurant or outdoor cafe for coffee or to split a snack, then continuing on. After about four stops we had circled back to the hotel and spent almost forty dollars on snacks!

The next day, we had an organized tour of the city in the morning, then came back to the hotel to roam around. In the late afternoon, we started down the hill through a beautiful park. The path wound down a very steep hill. I didn't realize how difficult it would be for me, since my foot/ankle brace limited my movement on hills. Unbelievably, it took me two hours to get down to the bottom of the park, and by then it was twilight.

I was scared. In New York City or Washington, D.C., you

didn't walk in city parks after dark. There were other people in this Madrid park, and hearing their voices made me even more fearful. We were completely lost, and it was too dark to tell where we were. Finally, we were so tired and hopeless, we approached a group of adults and children and asked for help. Stephanie had her Spanish-English dictionary, and managed to ask a few questions. They didn't know where our hotel was, but pointed us to where we could catch a taxi. To our surprise, the hotel was only a few blocks down the road.

The next morning we were up before daylight to start our bus tour of the country. There were about thirty other people on the tour with us. Even though I was a little slow getting on and off the bus—it was still hard for me to stretch as far as the first high step off the curb—I felt great. I had always loved to travel, to see new sights, meet new people, feel new places. I wanted to prove to myself and the world, that just because I had had a stroke, I didn't have to stay home and miss living my life.

We saw magnificent palaces, mosques, churches, villages, rolling green pastures, and the rock of Gibraltar. I was pleased with my ability to communicate without words to the local people we met. My gestures and expressions must have been universal. I was able to tell them about myself, find the men's room, order more coffee or get the check. I felt that I belonged there, without one word of Spanish (or English).

I couldn't always keep up with the tour group. One afternoon, I had trouble walking down a steep incline from a palace we'd visited to our bus. Everyone else had disappeared around the corner, but I couldn't go any faster. A few days earlier, the group had left behind one of the couples who hadn't returned on time. I didn't know whether they'd decided to stay and spend more time there, or had made a mistake. I didn't want the group to leave me and Stephanie behind. After helping me down to the bottom of the slope, Stephanie ran ahead to find the bus, and tell them to wait. The guide was a little frustrated with me, but the others didn't seem to care. I was so agitated by the effort and the anxiety, that it took most of the drive to the next city for me to calm down.

I'm glad that I had plenty of reading material about the places we visited. At each stop, a local guide would walk us through the sights. I had trouble keeping up on foot, and hearing what the guide had to say. By the time I'd catch up with the group, the guide was already half way through his or her description of the sight. Their accents were so strong and different, that I had trouble understanding them. And much of their commentaries were dates or other numbers or names that my aphasia blocked out. Stephanie tried to write down the key words in my notebook as the guide was speaking, and it helped a little. Even though I was frustrated by my disabilities, I was too stubborn to let them get in my way of absorbing and enjoying as much of Spain as I could.

Most of the others on the tour were very friendly and treated me as an equal, inviting us to sit with them at meals, commenting on the sights, asking about us, and looking after me. It was a very nice feeling, especially when Stephanie told the tour leader that it was my birthday, and everyone sang "happy birthday" to me. I was 41 years old. My birthday seemed more important to me, life seemed more precious. My life was different now, carrying around the burdens of a stroke, but I was doing what I loved to do—traveling, working, planning, setting goals, having hope for a better future.

Soon after we returned from Spain, Stephanie learned that her forty-year-old brother Stuart, was seriously ill with cancer. He was in and out of the hospital most of November, December and January. Stuart was living with their mother, and Stephanie spent a lot of time on the phone and at her mother's house helping. I missed her, but I knew how important it was for her to be there. I went with Stephanie as often as I could to visit her brother. Just because I had suffered a stroke, the world around me didn't stop, and I was an active participant for both the good times and the bad.

Stuart had cancer of the head and neck, and early in the treatment, they had to put in a trach tube in order for him to breathe. This meant that he couldn't talk unless he held the tab over the tube. After a while, the cancer locked his jaw shut and he couldn't talk at all. I understood some of what was happening to him, based on my own experience with the nurses and doctors, feeling helpless, and being robbed of my speech and ability to eat. The sad difference was that after my lowest point, I started to get better and stronger. After a round of radiation therapy, Stuart seemed to get a little stronger, then he went downhill quickly. By early February, the cancer had spread everywhere, he was in a lot of pain, and too frail to care for himself. Finally, they moved him from the hospital into a hospice.

The hospice offered him some much-needed comfort. He was in a single room, where his friends and family could visit easily. His room looked out on a garden with trees and birds. There was a large central living room where the nurses sometimes brought him to sit, and where we could sit and wait if he was busy with the nurse.

They also had a kitchen with an always-full pot of hot coffee. One evening when we were visiting Stuart, I was very tired and needed a cup of coffee. While the others chatted with him in his room, I went into the kitchen, poured myself a steaming cup, and carried it back with me. Stuart suddenly perked up. He gestured that he smelled my coffee and wanted some.

At that point, he couldn't swallow anything because the cancer had blocked his throat. He had given up a feeding tube, since the fluid kept seeping into his lungs and causing pneumonia and pain. Wanting to be helpful, and forgetting about his condition, Stephanie ran out of the room and came back with a cup of watered-down coffee. She put it to Stuart's lips. He gestured that he wanted hot coffee.

When she returned with another cup, he put one hand around it, and gestured with the other as if he were puffing on a cigarette. He seemed to come sparkling alive after so many weeks of being in a pain-fogged withdrawal. Tonight, my cup of coffee brought back a moment with the "old" Stuart. I felt that I had contributed something special to him and the family with this one inspiration. A few days later, on the day before

Valentine's Day, he passed away.

Soon after, I wrote a letter to my brother, who had moved to Hawaii. I put my heart and soul into it, describing my activities and feelings over the previous year. I told my brother about Stuart's death, about my trip to Spain, about my part-time work at the nonprofit group.

I wrote about my progress in physical therapy, that I could now walk all the way to the little grocery store by the main road, one mile from home. I had to sit and rest for a few minutes before walking the mile back. It was tiring, and my leg hurt when I got home, but this was solid, measurable progress.

As I was writing to my brother, I realized that I wanted to tell my story. I spent weeks carefully writing my experiences into a story, then sent it to a magazine for disabled people. They rejected it. The rejection didn't discourage me. Instead, it made me even more determined that someday I would sit down and write this book—to help me remember my feelings and understand what happened to me, and perhaps to help others who find themselves knocked down by life.

At the end of the summer, Stephanie wanted her mother to go to England, to visit their family in Manchester. We decided to meet her there, after spending a week touring Wales, home to our friends Arlene and Ron, who had greeted us at the beginning of our memorable trip to Ireland.

Much of Wales' modern history had revolved around the coal mining industry. I wanted to see a coal mine, not only to learn more about the country and its people, but also to satisfy something inside of me. I wanted to prove that, despite my disabilities, I could go anywhere and do anything. Ron was also a bit of an adventurer. Not far from their home in Cardiff, there was a site preserved by the government, with an extensive museum and a real coal mine open to tourists.

To get to the mine, you climbed into a rickety old elevator, more like a steel box on a pulley, that lowered you down a deep shaft into the tunnels. Stephanie and Arlene took one look and decided to sit out the tour in the tea room. Ron and I ventured ahead. For safety, we were outfitted with a helmet that had a lamp on it, connected to a battery pack they strapped around our waists with a heavy canister of oxygen and an oxygen mask.

The trip down was dim, but I didn't know how much I would miss even that faint light until a few minutes into the tunnels. The tunnels were wide, but very low, in some places maybe only five feet high. I had to bend down to walk, and to remember that the helmet and lamp added another few inches to my height. The walls were reinforced with curved beams, creating egg-shaped passageways. I banged my helmet a few times on the ceiling beams, knocking the lamp off. Thankfully, Ron helped me get it back into place.

My normal pace on dry, flat sidewalks was slower than the average person, but down here, in the dark, having to stoop, and then carefully pick my way around the wet, slippery coal-car rails and the muddy tunnel floor, I couldn't keep up with the tour. Ron stayed with me, and we made our way down treacherous slopes and up and over slimy bumps, to a fork in the tunnels. It was pitch dark in both directions, and we could not see nor hear a trace of the tour group. I was terrified. The terror somehow invigorated me. With Ron, I found my courage to keep going. My legs and back hurt from the extra weight of the battery/oxygen belt, and from stooping to avoid the low ceiling beams. It was hard to keep from falling, since my bad right leg pointed out and drooped, and even in my own living room I stubbed my toe often. Here it was worse. I was breathing very hard, from the cold, rank air, from the exertion, and from fear.

We wandered through the underground tunnels for what seemed like hours. Later Stephanie and Arlene confirmed that it had been at least two hours, more than double the time of a single tour.

We walked a few paces, listened until we heard people, tried to go in that direction, listened again, changed direction, listened again, then finally found the group. It wasn't until sometime later that I realized the tour guide was on his second or third tour when we stumbled upon him. As tired as I was, I was glad to follow the group and learn all the history of the mines: Where they had kept the miniature horses who spent their lives down in the mines pulling the coal carts, the engine room, the fan, where they had forced young boys to pull the ropes that kept the fans bringing in air. The thought that animals and people had spent their entire lives in this miserable blackness was almost as frightening as my own feelings of being lost earlier.

Of course, once we returned to the surface and sat with our wives for tea, we told them it was an interesting experience. Later, when Ron and Arlene came to the U.S. to visit us, I showed Arlene my journal, where I had written that I had been afraid. She asked Ron if he too had been afraid. He thought for a minute, and said, "yes." It had been an adventure for both of us. I felt that I had struggled and won one more battle with my disabilities. I had proven to myself that I was tough, and that life was not going to pass me by, no matter how difficult any one challenge might be.

I was feeling more sure about myself, more daring in the relative risks I would take, more anxious to prove that I could return to my favorite sports.

A few weeks after returning from England, I found a program sponsored by the county's recreation department which organized weekly team sports for disabled adults, including volleyball, basketball and other games at a local gym. What we were lacking in coordination and speed, because of our various handicaps, we made up in enthusiasm. We had a lot of fun. I could compete without worrying about my poor speech or dead right hand or awkward balance. For these games, it didn't matter that I was handicapped, I was moving around, breathing hard, and interacting with others who also enjoyed sports.

The recreation staff in charge of the program seemed to enjoy our spirit, and organized a number of challenging adventures for us. One was participating in a weekend ski trip co-sponsored by a large handicapped-skiing organization that had developed adapted ski equipment for all types of disabilities and had specially-trained instructors.

Before my stroke, since my early college years in Philadelphia, I had enjoyed skiing. I was an intermediate level skier and had taught Stephanie to ski. We had skied mostly at nearby slopes in western Pennsylvania and West Virginia. I missed it a lot.

As soon as I heard about the handicapped ski trip, I knew I wanted to go. I wanted Stephanie to go too, but she refused. She said she would be too nervous to watch me ski, and she didn't want to be stuck carrying my equipment and hers. She encouraged me to go, and I think I would have gone even without her blessings.

Enough people signed up to make the trip a "go," and I was really excited. This would be my first trip away from home without Stephanie. I had been alone at home when Stephanie travelled, so I knew I could take care of myself. But I was a little nervous about the trip. *Would I be able to get in and out of the shower by myself? Would I be able to explain to the recreational staff what help I needed if something went wrong? Would I really be able to ski?* I wanted to ski so much, that I pushed those fears out of my thoughts and pictured myself on the mountain, with the cold air blowing in my face, and the white snow shushing under my skis. I knew I could do it.

I rode to the ski resort with six of my fellow handicapped sportsters, and four recreational staffers in a county van driven by one of the staffers. We stayed in a motel about half-an- hour from the mountain. When we arrived, we had dinner, then went to our rooms. I was sharing it with one of the staffers. I didn't have any trouble getting ready for bed. I was really tired from the trip and the nervous anticipation, and quickly fell sound asleep.

The next morning, it seemed to take forever for everyone to get together and into the van. I realized that as bad as my disabilities were, others were worse. But our problems weren't going to stop us from enjoying life. Once at the ski lodge, the special program coordinator greeted us, introduced us to our individual ski instructors, and took us to pick out our ski equipment. My instructor helped me into a pair of ski boots and short skis. I wanted poles, but he said that I wouldn't need them.

Then I went with the group out onto the lower area of the "bunny"—the easiest beginners—slope. It took a long time to maneuver out of the lodge and up the little incline. I almost lost my balance a few times. But I was glad to be out on the snow. My instructor helped me climb a little way up, then ski down a few feet. Then he helped me grab onto the rope, towing us up to the top of the bunny slope. It was hard holding on to the rope with only one hand, and keeping my skis straight with my weak right leg. I felt that I was being pulled up the hill really fast, yet I remembered how slow it had seemed so many years ago, before my stroke.

At the top of the slope I let go of the rope, and tried to ski down the hill. About halfway down I lost my balance and fell. How to fall was the first thing I taught Stephanie about skiing. I knew it was part of the fun, so it didn't bother me. I needed a little help from the instructor to get my skis under me, then to stand up again. I managed to get the rest of the way to the bottom of the slope without falling.

After a few more runs up and down the bunny slope, my instructor said I was doing "fine," and asked if I wanted to take the chairlift to the top of a longer beginner's slope. I couldn't wait! We got into line, and I carefully slushed forward until we were the next in line for the chair. The instructor helped me get into place, and in an instant, the chair was under me, and somehow I was sitting in it, on my way up the slope. At the top, the instructor yelled to the attendant to hold the chair and they both helped me out and away from the lift.

I followed the instructor to one side of the ski area, and he explained how we were going to ski down. I was to place my hand on his forehead, as he skied backwards down the slope. My job was to steer him, and tell him when to avoid trees and light poles, while I skied facing forward. He locked my skis into a wedge, our skis touching, making an "x" shape. Then we started down. I was nervous about this working out, and it was a little hard for me to communicate. Mostly I'd just yell some sound, point my head and try to steer us out of the way when I saw us coming close to a tree or another skier. He was very patient and we made it all the way down the slope without falling or hitting anything. I was so proud of myself to be skiing again.

That summer, I went water skiing with the same special recreation group, south of Washington on a quiet part of the Potomac river, not too far from home. Unlike snow skiing which had been a long-time passion of mine, I had only been water skiing a few times before my stroke. But I wanted to prove that I could do anything, and looked for activities that would challenge me. Again, Stephanie said she couldn't bear to watch. So I went without her.

It was a beautiful sunny mid-summer afternoon by the time we were all assembled in our swimsuits on the small sandy beach of the river. The adapted water ski wasn't like the conventional water skis that fit on each foot. Instead, it looked like a short surfboard with a low chair, like a lawn chair, bolted onto it. The disabled person sat in the chair and held onto the tow rope, and a recreation staffer stood behind for balance and safety. It started on shore then was pulled by the motorboat a few yards out onto the river. The boat made a large circle, then returned to shore.

I was the second to the last person to take my turn. I hated having to wait so long for the ride. I watched as each of the others spilled into the water before making a complete circle. Their life vests and the staffer kept them afloat until the boat came back and pulled them to shore. Everyone fell in. I wasn't afraid of the water, because I knew I could swim, and felt safe with the life vest, but watching everyone fall made me more and more nervous.

Finally, it was my turn. The staffer helped me into the chair, and gave me the tow rope to hold. It was hard to adjust my grasp with just one hand, and my left hand was still not as strong as my right hand had once been. But before I could worry about it, the staffer asked if I was ready. I said, "yes," she gave the signal and we took off. I knew we weren't going very fast, since I had watched the others, but sitting there on the water, it felt like we were breaking speed records. I concentrated on my grasp on the tow line. I tried to keep myself balanced in the chair. I heard the staffer standing behind me yelling, "go," "go," "good job, Paul." I felt the water spraying me and squinted at the brightness of the sunlight. We made a complete large circle, then returned to shore—I had stayed afloat! I won! I didn't fall in! I wanted to go around again, but the staffer said there was another person still waiting to go.

As I climbed out of the ski chair, I felt great. I had proven to myself that I could do it, and I didn't fall in. I wished that others—employers, co-workers, friends—could have seen me that day. I wanted everyone to see that there is a real man under this stroke disguise.

The greatest fear faced by most people is the fear of standing before an audience to give a speech. While I took some risks to try snow skiing and water skiing, and going down into the Welsh mine was a frightening experience, my greatest challenge came when my urge to tell my story met my fear of standing up and speaking before a group. I always had stage-fright, even before my stroke. Now if I was under any pressure, my speech completely fell apart, and meaningless sounds came out instead of words. But my overwhelming need to tell people that a young man can survive a stroke and go on to live a full life drove me to beat this fear.

Through her contacts at work, Stephanie learned that the federal government had organized a panel of experts to draft guidelines for doctors and therapists on how to treat a person after a stroke. One of the panel's biggest controversies was the question: just how long after a stroke could a patient benefit from speech, physical and occupational therapy? They were debating weeks versus months. I was outraged. I was now in my sixth year of therapy, and still making progress. If I had stopped at six months, I would never have learned to sound out words, or walk without a cane, or balance the muscles in my arm to relieve the pain.

This was a special turning point for me, going from being helped to being the helper. I felt that my experiences could make a difference for other people who had had strokes. Stephanie signed us up to testify during a day of public hearings. I also urged my therapists to participate in the process. My physical therapist, Sally, agreed to testify, as did a speech therapist from the university where I was a guinea pig.

My presentation was only five paragraphs long, it took me about three minutes to read through it, but it felt like an hour. I wrote out the words and ideas that I wanted to cover, then Stephanie helped me put it in order and make it grammatically correct. We tested some words, and changed them for others that I could pronounce better. It took many weeks of preparation. First, I would practice some of the more difficult words from a list, then read the whole speech. I even practiced at my speech therapist's office in front of a small group of her other patients.

On the morning of the panel's hearing, Stephanie and I went to the hotel early to meet Sally for breakfast. It was an older hotel, and to my amazement, it wasn't handicapped-accessible. There were stairs everywhere throughout the lobby, in and out of the restaurants, in and out the meeting rooms, and even to get to the rest rooms. This was very difficult and time-consuming for me. How could a panel that was discussing strokes—a condition that leaves many people in wheelchairs or dependent on canes to get around—hold its only public hearing in an inaccessible hotel, when there were so many accessible locations available. This was a bad sign.

We were fifth on the list of ten speakers; only one other stroke survivor came to testify. When it was our turn, Stephanie went first. She described my situation and the six years of therapy we had paid for out of our own pockets. She made the point that effective long term speech, physical and occupational therapy can be affordable.

We wanted the panel to know that the medical community

had set up a vicious cycle that prevented most stroke survivors from getting the care they needed: doctors believed that progress was made only in the first few weeks after a stroke, so they don't prescribe therapy beyond two or three months. So, the insurance companies don't pay for more than two or three months of therapy. So most people don't get more than two or three months of therapy, and then they stop making progress, which reinforces the doctor's original belief that progress stops after a few weeks.

When Stephanie finished her comments, she introduced me. Here's what I said:

I am Paul Berger. I have two masters degrees, but my bad speech makes people think I am not smart. I am learning to speak with speech therapy, a tutor, a home-study grammar class, and by starting a Toastmasters club for head injury.

I go to PT, and exercise at home, and sometimes swim.

My stroke is different than old people. I am healthy except for my speech and right arm and leg. I work part time now, and want to work full time next year. Looking for work is hard, because phone calls are hard, and I cannot tell a boss how smart and hardworking I am.

My interests are: more and better computers, help with speech, and better job counseling.

I hope you will help the world to see and listen to people like me.

I was so nervous when I stood up to give this speech, my hand was shaking. My throat was dry as sandpaper, and I don't remember how I got through the three minutes. After I sat down, there was a long pause. The chairman of the panel was struck by my words, and said so. Then he and the other panelists asked a few questions, which Stephanie answered.

I remember that they were very impressed with my physical therapist Sally's testimony. She told them that she could even in one session, which was sometimes all her clients could afford, help them find some small measure of independence.

The panel asked her a number of questions, then asked her to send them more information.

My favorite comment from Sally was, "Sometimes it is the inexperienced therapist who 'plateaus,' not the patient."

Almost a year later, we got a copy of the panel's draft report to review. I was disappointed that they didn't make a stronger statement about long term therapy. But to their credit, they didn't suggest a specific time frame. They recommended that therapy should be pursued if the professionals believed that some progress can be made, and if the stroke patient showed progress. They also suggested giving the patient a chance to be reevaluated some time in the future, in case the immediate effects of the stroke or other health problems were too much or too distracting for the person to concentrate on therapy.

They also said that vocational rehabilitation, training to return to work, should be considered by doctors and professionals if appropriate for the patient. Reading this draft made me feel that I did have an impact, that my message was listened to, that other stroke patients might be encouraged to try long-term rehabilitation and hope to go back to work like me: That having a stroke didn't mean you had to give up.

The only part of the draft report that I didn't like was the section on recreation. It focused on playing cards, and one-handed card holders. I wrote back with a list of items I used for recreation: all of my tools for building model trains, floatation vest for swimming, adapted sports equipment for skiing. I wanted them to know that having a stroke didn't mean being left playing cards for the rest of your life, there were too many fun things to do with one hand.

Graduating From
the College of Courage
1993-1994

As I continued to make progress and managed a predictable routine, Stephanie had time to think about her own career development. She wanted to move up to the next level, but there weren't any opportunities where she was working.

I knew that she had put aside her own ambitions for the security of her current job, an anchor during the stormy times of my stroke and recovery. I wanted her to do well, to get ahead. That's what I wanted for myself, too. And knowing she'd make more money was nice, too. But I felt a little less than the "man of the house," being so dependent on her. Usually, we were partners in our financial decisions, but once in a while, to try to win her point, she'd remind me that she was supporting us. This hurt me more than she would ever know. I would get angry, and try to argue with the few words I could say, but I never let her know how bad I felt.

Of course, with the kind of luck we had, her "dream" job came with a catch: it was located in Baltimore, almost two hour's commute each way. She took the job anyway, because the opportunity to direct a large department for a health association was too hard for her to resist, and the salary and benefits seemed worth the physical and emotional costs of the long commute.

We talked about moving to Baltimore. I didn't want to move. I'd been in the Washington area now for fifteen years, had many friends, hobbies and clubs, and most of all, wanted to stay close to my speech and physical therapists. Stephanie's family was local, and she was active in a number of local organizations. It wasn't much of a discussion. I guess I might have been willing to move, but she didn't want to. She said that she'd eventually get another job back in the Washington area anyway.

So, for the next four years, she commuted to Baltimore.

148

Her days were very long. She'd get up before me, shower, make coffee, then wake me up. She'd be out of the house before I was moving. In the evening, she'd get home late, usually after seven p.m. She'd snack on the train, so she didn't want to eat dinner with me. I felt sorry for her long day and how hard it was for her. But most of all, I felt lonely. I missed her.

Soon after she started her new job, we remodeled our kitchen. The cabinets, appliances and counters were probably the age of the house, thirty years old, so it was time to modernize. There were some features we designed specifically to accommodate my disability: It was important to have a counter by the refrigerator to "land" food, so I could open the door, then put in or take out what I wanted. The dishwasher was on the left side of the sink, so I could load it with my left hand. (Stephanie is also left-handed, so this worked for both of us.)

And we installed a wall oven. This way I could open the oven, and lift things in and out, onto a nearby counter. Before, we had an oven under the stove, and when I bent down, my bad arm would swing into the hot oven. I tried to hold it by tying my apron over it, but that was a little uncomfortable, and sometimes my arm would slip out anyway. A few times I almost burned myself. I couldn't even check on how food was baking without worrying about hurting myself, so the wall oven was very important.

During the two weeks the workmen were remodeling, the house was a hazardous trap. There were appliances and boxes everywhere, and the furniture and carpets were covered with tarps. I stumbled and almost fell every time I tried to walk through the living room. It took longer to do everything, and I felt like a college kid with the coffee maker in the bathroom. But this was part of looking ahead, of making accommodations for my disabilities, of making it easier for me to do everyday tasks, to enjoy life. So the two weeks of chaos was worth it.

That September, I had a chance to again follow my spirit of adventure. Friends were stationed in Romania, and invited us to visit for a week. Before my stroke, I had visited poor countries in Central America and Eastern Europe. This trip was not a physical challenge, I was getting around okay. It would be a challenge to my senses and emotions.

When we landed in Romania, it was a little unsettling to see the armored military personnel on the tarmac. We had very specific instructions from Aaron and Sarah about which lines to go through and papers to show to get through customs. Our pockets were stuffed with tips for the locals: dollar bills and cigarettes.

In Aaron and Sarah's neighborhood, we saw long lines of people waiting for their government rations of bread. It was hard to find quality food, so Sarah had developed a network of contacts who called each other when they learned that a shop was carrying good chicken or fish. We went to a farmers market for fruit and vegetables, and it felt like we were walking through the middle ages.

In the street, raggedy children ran up to the car and begged for food. One girl said her mother was sick and needed chocolate. Sarah gave her a felt-tip pen, and the little girl shrieked with glee and ran off to show her friends.

One afternoon, Stephanie and I walked to a nearby park to see a museum dedicated to the agricultural history of Romania. There were little huts dotted through the park. At the park's small gift shop, we tried to find some souvenirs without luck.

We took a taxi, a tiny Romanian-made car, back to our friends' home. We paid the driver a dollar and gave him a few cigarettes as a tip.

I saw a lot of Bucharest, the capital, and some of the nearby areas. I was really struck by so many half-built buildings everywhere. The communists had started many projects, then ran out of money and never finished them. It looked like they'd been bombed.

Even the nicest places were depressing. When we ate at the best restaurant in town, catering to the international businessmen and visitors, Sarah and Aaron asked careful questions about the menu items and preparation, then explained which ones to choose from.

Our friends drove us to historic sites, into the countryside, to a beach where high ranking advisors to the former fascist leader had little homes. The farmers' homes had thatched roofs, looking hundreds of years old. Aaron explained that the farmers were doing well, they grew food they could keep or sell, and were better off than they were under the fascists, and doing much better than the city people. No one seemed to be smiling. It was as if a whole nation had suffered a stroke, and were lumbering to recover and adjust to their new lives.

Before we left, we wanted to bring home something that represented the local people. Sarah took us to an art shop. We saw some nice paintings, but most were dark and oppressive-looking. We wanted a painting of the city. The shop owner took us to a large one hanging in the window. Stephanie said it was a picture of Paris, not Bucharest, and pointed to the words on the bottom, "La Seine," the name of the river in Paris.

"The shop owner says even if you buy a painting from him, it will be taken away at the airport," Sarah explained. "It's against the law to take art out of the country. He says that the communists took a lot of their art, so a law was passed. He says there's a craft store down the block for tourists."

From the craft store, we picked out some beautifully hand-carved small wooden boxes, and a black leather vest for me. We still had a lot of Romanian money left, since we were required to buy it with American dollars, but we couldn't spend it. There was little to buy, the prices were low, and people barely survived there; they didn't have a consumer economy like ours.

When I got home, my speech therapist had me try to capture my experience and feelings in an essay. I realized that while my disabilities were a challenge for me, the Romanians I saw faced much greater suffering. I had a rich life before my stroke to look back on, rewarding experiences since my stroke, and the hope of future accomplishments. I was lucky. There were many people all over the world that were not as lucky as me. I had never been so sensitive to others before. I think the stroke gave me a new way of looking at life, and feeling grateful for what I had.

Now that seven years had passed since my stroke, I was beginning to plan for the big step: returning to work full time. I was tired of therapy, and bored with my part time job. My goal was to make the switch in the next year or so. I knew I'd have to start over in a low-level position, but I was convinced that if I could get a job with a bank, a financial company or a real estate developer, I'd be able to work my way up to a professional job.

In August, Stephanie and I attended one of the bi-monthly meetings of the local brain injury support group. The speaker was an employment counselor from a private agency that helped disabled people find work. She said that there were job openings at one of the big national mortgage companies, but didn't have any clients who were interested. I really perked up. Afterwards, we asked to meet about hiring her agency to help me find a job. She understood that I wanted to spend the next year researching my options, completing my therapy goals, and preparing for the transition. She was very encouraging and I felt great about my plans.

Two months later, I had my meeting with the counselor. And it wasn't to plan for next year.

The board of the nonprofit group had decided to "outsource" the financial department. Most of the people in my department, from my boss down through most of the clerks— including me—were given a month's notice. I couldn't believe that I'd been laid off again. I thought I'd have the choice of when to leave. I wasn't ready to change my comfortable routine yet.

I had to make an important decision, and it wasn't easy. Should I look for another part-time job, so I could continue with my speech and physical therapy, since I was still making noticeable progress, or should I start the search for my new career and a full time job now. Stephanie and I talked it out. I couldn't see myself going through two job searches in a year. And there were many more full-time jobs out there, so my chances would be better. Most of all, I was really tired of therapy.

I called the counselor and told her that my plans had changed and asked for her help. She said they had an arrangement with the Department of Rehabilitative Services, and asked if I had returned there to reopen my case. That was the last thing I wanted to do, and told her about my unhappy experiences with them. I said that I would pay her company out of my own pocket, if they could accept private clients. She agreed and about a week later, I went to her office with my file of work samples, references, resumes and dreams.

My goal was modest: to find a job a step higher than a clerical position. I knew I could be a research assistant, helping to find information. I knew a lot about the commercial real estate industry and related financial interests. I though I'd be a good candidate for her contact at the national mortgage company. She said she'd get things moving, and assigned my case to one of her work specialists, Karie.

As part of my severance package, the nonprofit group paid my salary for a month, and signed me up to attend sessions of the Multiple Sclerosis (MS) Society's job strategy program for disabled people. This was the second time I had enrolled in this program. The first was just after leaving my city government job, about six years earlier. Back then, I'd had too little speech to participate in the discussions. This time around, I was very active, and could usually get my point across. The program lasted for twelve weeks, and attending the sessions downtown twice a week really helped me through this difficult period.

The MS program staff and Karie helped me rewrite my resume and improve my interview notebook, which now included samples from my accounting work at the nonprofit group, as well as my references and work samples from my volunteering at the association and my government job. They helped me focus on what I could do, not on what I couldn't do. I didn't think about the professional skills I'd lost. I concen-

153

trated on the research, math, bookkeeping and computer work I could do now.

Inside, I knew that I had earned two masters degrees, and had helped the city government organize local builders to complete a number of important office buildings, department stores and hotels. The senior levels of the department chose me to help with these projects because they knew I could get the job done. This was still part of who I was. And I was a hard worker, mature, loyal, with an excellent attendance record since my stroke. I was certain that employers would want me.

Stephanie helped me find ads in the newspaper for interesting jobs, and drafted form cover letters, using our computer word processing software, so I could do most of the work. I printed out and mailed letters and resumes to a hundred companies, sending copies to Karie. She'd call to find out more about the job, explain who I was, what I could do, and try to arrange an interview. By the time my last day of work at the nonprofit group came, I was in high gear with my job search.

I had a few interviews for interesting jobs that I knew I could do, sometimes going alone, sometimes with Karie. Most of them were disasters. The interviewers asked me unkind and probably illegal questions about my disabilities, and didn't believe that I could do the work. I shared these experiences during my sessions at the MS Society. It helped to talk to others who were going through the same thing. They made me realize that I didn't want to work for such narrow-minded people anyway.

Then came a series of telephone conversations between Karie and a company in Arlington. She arranged for an interview, and went with me. I did most of the talking. I presented my notebook full of work samples, and tried to explain how I could contribute to their company. It was a small consulting firm which compiled data on the utility industry. While it wasn't exactly what I wanted, I was interested in public utilities, and the people I met seemed nice. I thought there would be a chance for advancement as I learned more about their work.

They seemed ready to give me the job that day, because the

conversation quickly turned to logistical questions about when I could start and accommodations. Karie mentioned that they would be eligible for a tax credit, but they declined, and said they would start me as a Technical Assistant, at a salary that was considerably higher than what I had earned at the nonprofit group. I was so excited to see my dream come true.

I started the second week in December, just in time for Christmas celebrations. My desk was set up in the office of my supervisor, a young engineer from another country. They were using an older computer network system and software that I'd have to learn. Stephanie found some self-study disks and booklets from a used computer store that I practiced at home and at work.

I finished my first assignment in three days, then pitched in on a big project with very tight deadlines. I worked that Saturday, helping to enter data. I was very slow, because it was all new to me, but I managed to finish my part. I was proud to be a member of a professional team.

That New Years Eve, I really celebrated. I was finally going to make it! I was finally back on track to build a new career. I felt great!

Over the weeks that followed, I had a few interesting projects, but mostly I was waiting for something substantial to come along. My supervisor gave me articles from journals to read and file. I even analyzed one for him to show that I could learn and understand the new information.

One of the other managers gave me a project to audit. I had to verify data that were entered into her database. It was nice to have her show support for me, and I enjoyed doing it. When I completed that project, I realized that I didn't have an ongoing task that was my own. I was starting to get concerned about this, so I made a list of things that I thought I could do, and showed it to my supervisor. He was never one to use a lot of words, but this time he didn't say anything about my list. It was really frustrating. He didn't acknowledge my initiative or needs. I didn't know what to do next. How could I talk to him about it, if he didn't say anything to me?

I asked Karie what to do. She said that from time to time, she had called my supervisor to offer assistance. He was nice to her, and always assured her that he had things "under control." After I called her, she called him, and the next thing I knew, we were meeting with my supervisor and one of the senior partners.

I was unprepared for the turn of the discussion. They said they wanted to keep me employed with their firm, but that they didn't think my skills were strong enough to do the projects they'd expected for my current starting pay level. I was upset about this, since I did everything they gave me, and no one told me that there had been anything wrong with my work. Nor had they said anything to Karie. Plus, I was begging my supervisor to give me more. This wasn't fair. I knew I could do more, to earn the salary they were giving me. This wasn't my fault. But more than anything, I wanted to keep this job. The scars of being laid off by my previous employers were too fresh and sore.

At the end of the meeting, I had reluctantly agreed to a cut in pay back down to the level that I'd been earning at the non-profit group. In return, I'd have ongoing clerical duties, including collecting, recording and reporting time sheets from everyone, and verifying the phone and fax logs, to help in billing the clients. They told me that I'd be doing the graphics work, making up charts and graphs to go into their proposals and reports using computer software. Another staff person would train me. They also gave me the task of picking up the mail, and occasionally acting as a delivery person.

I was sad that they'd pegged me back to the lowliest clerical level. But I still thought that I'd have the chance to prove myself and work my way up to a higher level. I liked the people, I liked the utility industry, and I liked the full-time paycheck, even if it would be less.

For the next few months, I settled into a pleasant routine, learning my new responsibilities, and the new software. At first, it took most of the week for me to sort through and enter the time sheets. After a few months, I was able to complete that task in a day-and-a-half. I enjoyed getting up from my desk in the mornings to get the mail, and going out occasionally to pick up documents downtown, a nice break from the boring clerical work.

About six months later, Karie's group held its annual recognition reception for employers. My company was recognized for hiring me, and Stephanie and I were invited to address the group to present my perspective on looking for work and finding it. James Brady, Reagan's former press secretary, was the keynote speaker. I was excited and nervous to be on the same program with a national figure, and once again to be standing before a crowd to speak. Knowing that I'd done this before didn't give me much confidence. That deep down fear of speaking was still a challenge.

Stephanie helped me write what I wanted to say. I practiced first reciting each of the words so I'd remember how to pronounce them correctly. Then I read the full speech. I practiced every evening, reading it out loud, thinking I'd said the words right, then feeling frustrated when Stephanie corrected me. When I thought I was saying one word, what actually came out of my mouth was either a different word, or the "filler" that I always used unconsciously, the word, "like." I could put together a whole complicated thought in my mind, then when I tried to say it, all that would come out was a string of "like, like, like..." It was very frustrating for me, and I'm sure just as frustrating to my listener.

I wanted to be perfect, but I still had aphasia.

The night of the reception I was very nervous. Three people from my office came, since they were being honored for hiring me, and they had placed an ad in the program guide saying, "Paul Berger, we are very proud of you!"

I'd wanted to meet James Brady. He was an inspiration to me, watching him recover over the years. Unfortunately, he only had the time to deliver his speech then leave.

When it was my turn, I walked up to the podium with very shaky legs. I was sweating and trying really hard to control myself. My throat was very dry.

My name is Paul Berger. I had a stroke 8 years ago. I worked part time for 7 years and had speech and physical therapy. I was laid off in October. I decided enough therapy, and my employment specialist helped me find a full time job.

My employment specialist came to my house and my old job to see what I can do. She phoned employers and set interviews. I saw an ad in the Washington Post for a job. She phoned the job. I went on an interview with my employment specialist, and the employer said, okay, we will try Paul.

Now, I work full time for an energy consulting group as a Technical Support Assistant. I am a hard worker, and I like the other workers at the group because all are hard workers.

Thank you.

This short speech took me almost five minutes to present, and it felt like five hours! Somehow I made it back to my seat in the front row, and wiped the sweat off my forehead. That was so much harder than I thought it would be. But I'm glad I did it. It felt so good to be able to tell other employers that a disabled person like me should be on their staff. Just because speaking is difficult for me, doesn't mean that I'm stupid or unable to do many productive tasks. Having the use of only one hand and limping when I walk doesn't stop me from finding ways to get things done.

I started to breathe normally again. I noticed that Stephanie was just about to finish her presentation. I don't remember hearing her speak. I guess I was too busy trying to calm down. Afterward, she said I did a good job, and others congratulated me. Enjoying the refreshments, I thought to myself, I like my life.

A few weeks later, Stephanie and I were invited by my physical therapist to speak to a professional meeting of other therapists, to give them the "client's perspective." They wanted to know how I managed to conquer my stroke. It made me

158

think back over the years, to try to understand what I did and what I learned that might help others fight back, and help their therapists support them in their struggles.

I developed a list, and Stephanie typed it out to distribute at the meeting. This made me a little less nervous about being "perfect" when I had to deliver my speech. When I wrote out the list, I realized that I had accomplished a lot. I wanted other people to know about it, not just to ease my pain, but to help others who might be suffering through their own crises, to give them hope, to let them know that if I could do it, they could too.

About that time, former President Richard Nixon had a massive stroke and died. In the newspaper's health section, there was an article explaining strokes, and what had happened to Nixon. The neurologist interviewed for the article said that if he had lived, he might have seen improvements for three to six months following the stroke. When I saw that statement, I was really angry. This nationally-respected newspaper was perpetuating the old myth that stroke survivors only benefited from short-term therapy. Stephanie agreed to write a letter to the editor to clear things up. We took issue with the short time frame and explained my progress:

In two years, Paul had a vocabulary of about 100 words. In five years, he could form simple sentences and had a vocabulary of about 1,000 words. In seven years, he could form more complicated sentences and had regained many complex, multi-syllabic words.

By six months, he could stand and walk a few steps with another person's assistance. By nine months, he could stand and walk about a block with a cane; by two years, about six blocks with a cane. By five years, he could do a mile with a cane and a few rest stops. By seven years, he could walk a mile nonstop without a cane.

A few weeks later, they published it! We both felt a special kind of satisfaction that we'd succeeded at sharing some important information in a place where it might make a difference. Maybe a few doctors might actually read this letter and decide to prescribe a longer course of therapy for their patients.

Many of our friends and colleagues called to say they'd read the letter. A few strangers took the time to find our phone number and call us. Some wanted help, more information, or the names of my therapists. One of my therapists called and said that she'd put a copy of the letter on the bulletin board in her hospital's rehab department, and many family members had told her it gave them hope that their loved ones would be able to conquer their strokes, too.

The editor of a physical therapy magazine also saw the letter to the editor, and called me. She wanted to interview me, Stephanie and my physical therapist for a story in her magazine on the benefits of long-term physical therapy. She came to our house, took our pictures, and wrote a very flattering in-depth article about me entitled, "Long-Term Therapy Enables Stroke Victim to Regain Independence." I was the "centerfold" of the magazine that month!

It made me feel proud that my story might help therapists do more, and give hope to their patients. I wanted to make the therapists know that they shouldn't give up. They should believe in their patients and push them and find new ways to solve their problems, just like I did with my therapists. Giving other people hope and support made me feel that something good could come from my experience. Of course I never wanted to have a stroke and be a role model, but if this was my life, then I wanted to feel that I could do something important with it.

That summer, Stephanie and I decided to throw a party to thank our family, friends and therapists for their support over the past eight years. I really had a deep, happy feeling as we worked on planning the party. I owed these people so much, and I felt I might not have been able to get back my life if they hadn't been there to help me.

It was also a chance to finally feel that I was closing that chapter of my life, and starting toward new goals. The biggest difference between therapy and going to school was that school had clear milestones—the beginning and ending of semesters, final exams, the end of the school year, and graduation. In therapy, I had periodic evaluations, and I knew that I was making progress, marked by how far I could walk with or without a cane, or by how many new words I could say. But it just went on and on, and I often felt that I'd never see an end.

Stephanie said that for all the work I did in speech, physical and occupational therapy over a period of eight years, I should have earned a Ph.D. in each! That became the theme of our party: a June graduation from therapy.

We found a calligrapher to design a diploma for me. At first she didn't want to get involved in a "counterfeit" diploma, until we explained the purpose and she read the text that Stephanie had written. When she saw it was from the "University of Survival, College of Courage," with honorary degrees in speech, physical and occupational therapy, she was more than happy to help me, and even designed a "seal of courage" in gold foil. The diploma said:

> *Following the completion of eight years of consecutive, uninterrupted, diligent, persistent, muscle-aching, mind-stretching, obstinate, tenacious, industrious, assiduous work and with the gracious recommendation of the Faculty [each of my therapists] hereby confers upon Paul E. Berger the degrees of Honorary Doctorate of Physical Therapy, Doctorate of Occupational Therapy, Doctorate of Speech and Language Pathology, with all the rights, privileges and honors thereunto appertaining, having reclaimed his lost speech, numbers, reading, writing, walking, and all manner of activities and pursuits. In witness whereof we have hereunto affixed our signatures and the Seal of Courage in Virginia on this twenty-fifth day of June, nineteen hundred and ninety-four.*

We picked a nice Italian restaurant in Old Town Alexandria, about a twenty minute drive from home, for the party. They had a party room that would hold a hundred guests. It made me feel good to fill the room.

161

We tried to make the party look formal with fancy invitations we made on our home computer using an engraving font. We used the same font to make formal programs for the party and place cards. We also placed a small ceramic cup with a chocolate "turtle" at each seat. The turtle represented my own struggle like the old story about the rabbit and the turtle who entered a race. The rabbit hopped around and got distracted and never made it to the finish line, while the turtle, like me, slowly plodded on toward his goal and won the race.

We hired a video-photographer to record the whole party. I wanted to be able to remember the good times, since so much of my recovery was marked with problems and frustrations. The videographer was very touched by my story and anxious to make it feel like a real graduation. When he returned the tape, he had dubbed in "pomp and circumstance" music! He also captured individual messages from everyone there, which when I saw the tape, made me know that this party was the right thing to do.

Graduations are not complete without a lot of speeches, and a keynote speaker. Stephanie did a nice job as the master of ceremonies, introducing everyone to each other, reciting special thank-you's to many of the guests, and holding the microphone when I gave my speech:

> *Thank you all. Today I graduate from 8 years of therapy—speech and physical therapy to full time work. This party is to say thank you very much to the therapists and tutor for the long time of help. Mary, Sally, Jenny, Becki, Barbara, Janey. Over the years, I remember I was a model for Mary and Sally's classes— lots of therapists watching me in my swimsuit. Janey helped me with my wheelchair—but, one rainy day she accidentally pushed me off the ramp into the bushes— me holding the umbrella. Jenny hit me with her pen when I was wrong and came to my office at lunch for speech therapy. Becki made me write lists of new words. Barbara tutored numbers over and over and over. My friends helped me build my model trains.*
>
> *All my friends are great—talking to me when it is*

hard. Stephanie's Mom and family—talking to me. My
Mom and Dad—phone every week—I love you. To my
dear wife, Stephanie, thank you for your devotion, love
and support. Tomorrow, new job, new goals, hobbies,
more dinners and fun!

I was very nervous standing up in front of an audience to give my speech, but as I talked, my friends were first quiet, then they laughed at the right places. I didn't pronounce every word right, but I know that they understood why I wanted to celebrate with them.

Then my speech therapist, Jenny, talked about how hard it was from the very beginning for me: how I couldn't process the difference between "yes" and "no," and how every step of the speech therapy was such a challenge because my stroke had been so severe. She hadn't thought that she'd be providing long-term therapy, and the years just passed so quickly. Running out of prepared materials in the first year, Jenny and her assistants developed all of my worksheets and homework by hand. She said that some day soon she was planning to write up all the data from five full files on me, and present it as proof that someone can make impressive progress.

Then my occupational therapist Mary told the story of how I helped to get handicapped parking spaces in the medical building where her office was located, and how Janey and I would leave printed notes on the windshields of non-handi-capped cars parked in the spaces saying that a handicapped person was late for his appointment because you parked here. Mary said that she was inspired by my determination and ability to smile; to have a sense of humor throughout the difficult and sometimes painful therapy sessions.

After dinner, we had the signing ceremony, where each of the therapists signed my "diploma," then Becki, one of my speech therapists, read it out loud. The best surprise came last, when Stephanie had arranged for our Congresswoman to attend and give the "keynote" speech. She had always remembered me from that summer I volunteered one morning a week filing walking cards when she campaigned for state delegate five years earlier. We both had come a long way since then.

In her speech, she called me her "hero," for my courage in overcoming my stroke. And to show her respect, she gave me a letter of tribute written on her Congressional letterhead, and a flag that had been flown in my honor over the U.S. Capitol. I didn't have the words to thank her, and it was a little embarrassing when she hugged me in front of everyone. But as the evening came to an end, and people were telling me how much they had enjoyed the party, I really felt that I had conquered the world, and was ready for whatever the future would bring.

Part 3:
Conquering the Dream

Being My Own Boss
1995

I wish I could say that, as the months passed, my job responsibilities grew and I was taking steps up to higher levels of satisfaction. The engineer who was supposed to train me to do the graphics work never seemed to have time. My supervisor taught me the basics, and I practiced on the lessons that came with the two software packages. A few times I asked my supervisor when I'd start doing the graphics work, as they had promised. It was a time-consuming job, so it made sense from a financial perspective to have me do the work, not an engineer. Eventually, my supervisor told me that even though I had learned the program, I would not be doing any graphics. He didn't explain, and I guess he didn't understand how disappointed I was. This job had become a big disappointment.

I wasn't happy, but I wanted to stay. It was an easy routine, and I liked having a place to go, and getting the full-time paycheck. I still had hopes that eventually I could convince them to give me more interesting things to do. And it always made me feel good to walk from the parking garage to my office, across the pedestrian bridge high over the traffic and stop to look at the view. In good weather, I could see up and down the Potomac river: Georgetown University, the shops in Georgetown, and even the tops of the Washington Monument and Capitol building. It was a wonderful view.

Maybe it was just bad timing. The company was having some tough breaks. Some of the contract renewals and new contracts that they had counted on didn't come through. The Republicans had just won the majority in Congress and many consulting companies in the Washington, D.C. area were suffering from cutbacks in government contracts.

There were a lot of highly skilled people finding themselves out of work. Some people left my company, and one of the senior, founding partners decided to cut down on his hours. Then they told me that they couldn't afford to keep me full time. They reduced my hours to two days a week, and suggested that I start looking for another job.

As unhappy as I had been, this news was devastating. I thought that I had control over staying or going. But they took that away from me. Again. I was being laid off, losing again. I was being thrown away. I wasn't worth anything to them but a few hours a week. After all the years of therapy, and the anticipation of returning to "normal" when they hired me, I had crashed again. Disabled, unwanted, angry at them, angry at myself.

I called Karie and asked for help.

When looking for a job, all the experts tell you to network: talk to everyone you know and go places where you can meet new people who might point you to a job opportunity. A few months earlier, I had joined the local business revitalization association and attended their lunches and evening receptions. I met some nice people, and developed a deeper appreciation for the area. At their next luncheon meeting, I talked to everyone I could about looking for a job. It wasn't easy, because of my aphasia. And when I was a little nervous, it was even harder to form a complete sentence. One of the attendees suggested that I join his Toastmasters club, as a way to practice speaking—especially for job interviews—and to network.

I really liked the idea. Before my stroke, I had attended a few meetings of a Toastmasters club associated with my city department. The club that I was invited to join met at a nearby restaurant on Monday nights for dinner and speeches. The members were from all walks of life, brought together for the common purpose of improving their ability to speak. As I got to know the others, I started to relax and enjoy myself. It made me feel good to know that I wasn't alone in wanting to improve my speech. These people weren't disabled but they wanted the same thing. Maybe my language skills were a lot worse than theirs, but they were just as nervous as me when they went to the front of the room to speak.

The first speech you give in the Toastmasters program is called an "Ice Breaker." It's a chance to tell the group a little about yourself. I wanted the club to know that I was a smart person, with a professional background, and not to judge me by my language problems. I spent a lot of time working on my speech, with Stephanie's help. I learned to say some new words, and memorized as much of it as I could.

Even with all the practice, it was still very hard. When I read a sentence, it sounded flat. I couldn't make my voice rise and fall to signal the end of a sentence or emphasize punctuation. I tried, but I just couldn't relearn how to do it. In high school, I had been in the choir, and had had a very good singing voice. After my stroke, I lost my singing abilities, I couldn't raise my voice, and I couldn't whisper either.

When it was my turn to give my Ice Breaker, I tried to be perfect, to make eye contact, to sound upbeat. I really wanted to win the ribbon for "best speech"—another way that the Toastmasters program motivates its members. I was very disappointed when I didn't win. I didn't know if I'd ever win as best speaker, but I wasn't going to stop trying for that trophy.

Memorizing key points about my life and career for this speech turned out to be very helpful. There were many times during interviews and meeting new people that I used some of the phrases I'd learned.

For two months, Stephanie helped me search the "help wanted" ads for a new job. Since I had so many years of work experience following my stroke, and good luck in previous job searches, I felt confident that I'd be able to find something good. We responded to every accounting, general clerical and research assistant job we could find, as well as anything related to real estate: office work for mortgage companies, rental management, and construction. I had three different resumes highlighting different aspects of my career, listing the eight different computer programs I used, and the various computer, accounting, research, and clerical duties I performed in my previous jobs. I spent most Sunday afternoons and evenings faxing cover letters and resumes to prospective employers, in all, more than two hundred. Karie followed up on as many as she could, and made calls to her other contacts.

I had seventeen interviews for a whole range of jobs. In most job search books, the big step is getting in the door for an interview. I quickly learned that having the interview wasn't enough. Most of the people who interviewed me were nice, but some asked very unkind questions about my disabilities. And even though I showed them my notebook of work samples, including spreadsheets, time sheet tallies, and other computer work, they didn't seem to believe that I could do the job. Every job, even the lowest levels that had no customer contact, seemed to require excellent speaking abilities. They told me that my speech was too poor to qualify. I asked to see the job description during one interview, and the employer got very upset and mumbled about how the description was changing.

I felt really bad. I hated having to interview for such low-level jobs, and felt even worse when they refused to believe that I was qualified. I knew I could do those jobs and more. I had done these jobs for other employers. My rotten speech just killed my chances to prove myself. I was on an emotional roller coaster, feeling very "up" when I was getting ready for an interview, then very "down" just after it. Sometimes, I would come home from an interview and feel that I had a good chance for the job, then not hear anything. Karie would call and get all kinds of excuses why someone else was given the job.

I tried different approaches, sometimes taking Karie with me on the interview, sometimes going alone. One time Karie had a prior commitment, and sent another counselor. We had planned to meet at a cafeteria about half-an-hour before the interview, just to review notes, and pump up my self-confidence. This job looked like a great fit for me, and I was excited about it. One of my friends had met the senior associate and would call on my behalf after the interview.

The other counselor never showed, so I went to the office by myself. I didn't want to be late. A few minutes later, the counselor arrived all out of breath. I was really upset, and very distracted by the whole incident. I needed to calm down and be at my best for this. When the supervisor came to see me, she told me that she had tried to reach me to reschedule our interview, since they were remodeling the office, and she didn't feel well. The counselor was left in the reception area, and I went with the supervisor for a brief interview. I was encouraged when she introduced me to her boss, the senior associate.

Despite my friend's phone call and the counselor's follow-up, someone else got the job. Stephanie, Karie and I tried to understand what was going wrong. I couldn't accept that I was facing the worst kind of discrimination. I was angry and disappointed, but I didn't want a lawsuit, I wanted a job.

One of the biggest problems was very bad timing. The shift in power in Congress had unseated thousands of clerical as well as professional workers from their Capitol Hill jobs and from companies that did business with the Democrats. For even the lowest positions, I was facing very skilled competition—sometimes ten or fifteen other applicants—most of whom had college degrees and good language skills.

I was getting more angry and depressed. I needed to make something happen. I needed a new battle plan, because I was losing this war. I decided to find another employment company. Maybe a fresh start with different counselors would be the answer. Stephanie suggested that instead of paying an hourly amount for the number of hours spent by the counselor—which just rewarded process but not results—we should offer a flat fee, equal to about one-month's work (what we'd paid in a month to the other firm). The new counselor would get his fee only when he placed me in a job. If he made one call and placed me, he'd get the full amount.

He looked at my resume and work samples, we talked for a long time about my previous work and my realistic expectations for my next job. He said that he knew some employers who would be a good match, and would make some calls. In the meantime, I was to continue sending out resumes to job openings, and sending him copies for follow-up. We both felt that I'd be in a new job soon.

A month passed, and he hadn't been able to set me up with even one interview. I was going crazy. I wanted to work. I needed to work to feel like a man. As the weeks passed, I felt more and more like a little bug. I kept busy by doing household chores, running errands, shopping, taking walks, and even attending monthly meetings of the local chapter of retired federal workers. I was having a tough time trying to feel positive.

Stephanie suggested that I needed a break and should visit my parents in Florida. She was very busy at work and didn't want to take time off. I think she needed a little break, too. It was late October, and starting to get cold and gray in Washington, and I knew it would be warm and sunny in Florida. I called my parents and they said that they would be delighted to see me. In the next two weeks, I felt happy making my plans and thinking about what I'd do when I got to Florida. Just having something nice to look forward to made me feel better.

I was a little nervous. This would be my first trip traveling alone since my stroke. I'd have to get to the airport, manage my luggage, check in, get to the right gate on time, and get on the airplane without Stephanie's assistance. This was a challenge, and I was ready to prove myself. Since I was going to Florida, I decided to pack "light." My parents wouldn't care if I wore the same shirt more than once. This way, I could fit everything I'd need into one carry-on bag. When I traveled with Stephanie, we usually took two bags: a larger one with most of our clothing, and this little carry-on, with a pull-out handle and wheels. Stephanie took the larger one, and I usually was in charge of the carry-on, so I knew I could manage it.

Since Stephanie was at work the morning I left for Florida, I had to take a taxi to the airport by myself. I had a note card with all the flight information written on one side so I could easily refer to it. I showed the taxi driver the card, so he knew to take me to Dulles Airport, and to the right airlines. On the back of the card was my parents' address and phone number in Florida, as well as my home address, phone, Stephanie's work phone, and directions to my house to show the taxi driver when I returned.

I had my boarding pass, and just the one carry-on bag, so when I came into the terminal, I looked for a monitor that

171

would tell me what gate my flight was leaving from. It took a few minutes for me to sort out the information on the busy screen. When I found my flight and the gate number, I started to relax a little. I was going to be just fine by myself. I went through the security check; the guard helped me lift my luggage onto the belt. Soon I was on the shuttle to the mid-field terminal. As we passed the other planes, I felt myself getting excited about the trip. I found my gate, checked in, and waited for the boarding call.

Getting on the plane and in my seat was a more of a challenge. I had a little trouble in the narrow aisle, and had to ask another passenger to lift my carry-on into the overhead compartment. Once I was settled into my seat, and the plane took off, I felt my emotions flooding in.

I was my own man, traveling by myself. I felt like I could do anything I wanted. For a few moments, I forgot about my disabilities. I forgot about my job search. I left my problems behind. Ahead of me was a week of sun and relaxation and pampering by my parents. The rest of the trip went without a hitch. My parents met me at the airport, took me to lunch, and we had a very nice time. I missed Stephanie, but we talked every night.

One night when I called her, she had skimmed through the weekday paper's "help wanted," and found an ad for a "computer graphics subcontractor," to work from home. She had called the number and discussed the requirements. They would train me to use their software to build computer graphics models of everyday items. Stephanie suggested that I could do this to keep busy while I was looking for a job.

I liked that idea. It made the rest of my trip feel even better. While I sat by the pool in the sun, enjoying the warm air and my parents' company, I forgot the humiliation of seventeen interviews and rejections for lowly clerical jobs. I needed this trip to show myself that I was still a special person. I gave myself a new challenge, traveling alone, and conquered it. And now I had something new and interesting to look forward to when I got home. I relaxed and recharged.

The week after I returned from Florida, Stephanie and I attended an orientation session for the computer graphics sub-contracting work, downtown, after dinner. Six other people attended with us. The presenter gave us a low-key sales pitch on the business. They were building a collection of computer graphics images, "models," of every day objects, like automobiles, furniture and kitchen appliances, that they'd package and sell as "clip art."

He explained that the company didn't have the capital to hire a staff of computer graphics artists and buy them computer equipment, so they'd rely on freelance subcontractors to do the work at home and buy one project at a time from us. The presenter said that he was looking for people who had computer experience, were good at math, and could take photos of the items we were going to model.

There were some good questions after the demonstration, and a discussion of how much we could expect to earn, how much their software cost, and expenses for other equipment (like a 35 mm camera). He distributed a three-page contract and told us to think about it. When we were ready to sign the contract and purchase the software, he'd schedule us for a three-session training course.

I wanted to read the contract and talk to Stephanie about it, but I was pretty sure that I could do this and would sign on. The software wasn't expensive, about what we'd paid for some of the business software we had on our home computer. This felt like a real opportunity, not a scam.

I thought that this was the kind of work that I could do well. It didn't require any writing or speaking skills. The modeling required some algebra and geometry skills, being able to locate objects on three dimensional planes, skills I'd kept. Some strokes wipe out people's ability to see things on a map or in three dimensions, but mine didn't. I'd been assembling complex train models, and finding employers in all parts of the area with just a map.

A few days later, just before Thanksgiving, we called the presenter and made arrangements to pick up the software and drop off our contract and payment. Stephanie wanted to use the long holiday weekend to install the program, play with it, and see how much I could do before the first training session. We also got permission for Stephanie to attend as my note-taker. We explained my disability to the presenter, and he was very understanding.

We installed the program and I tried the first lesson. It went well until I came to a step where I had to click the mouse, and hold down two other keys. I couldn't do it with one hand, and I couldn't control my right hand well enough to help.

I couldn't believe it. I thought I'd finally found an interesting, challenging, worthwhile opportunity, and I was about to lose it because of one step in the process. I got very upset. But Stephanie wouldn't give up so quickly. She left a message for the presenter to see if there was an alternate key combination, since many software programs have multiple ways of accomplishing each command.

"Let's go to the computer store," Stephanie said. "If they don't have something that can help, maybe they can build or order something special for you."

It was worth a try. The store was crowded with holiday shoppers, but soon we found the answer: a keyboard that had the mouse function built in as a "touchpad" next to the very keys required to accomplish the step. I practiced the combination on the keyboard in the store. I was so relieved. We bought the new keyboard, took it home and installed it. I finished the lesson and made a list of questions to ask the presenter.

The next hurdle was taking pictures of the objects that I wanted to model. The photos would then be scanned onto a computer disk, so I could use them in the program. With only one hand, taking pictures was difficult, and since cameras are built for right-handed people, I had to hold the camera upside-down to reach the buttons. This wouldn't work for the program. The coordinates for building the models depended on exact settings of the camera, which I couldn't do upside down.

I felt that some outside force was trying to stop me from being happy and successful. I was anxious and frustrated by my disabilities. But after feeling sorry for myself for a little while, I turned to focus on the solution. And it wasn't hard: attach the camera to a tripod. This would keep the camera steady. And although setting up the tripod and getting the camera mounted was a little tricky for me, once it was done, I was able to make all the adjustments needed to take pictures according to the software's specifications.

Stephanie's original idea was that this project would keep me busy until I found a full-time job. But I was convinced that I could earn the same as from a part-time job, and build it up as I got more skilled. I decided to end my job search, which wasn't too hard, since I hadn't had an interview in weeks.

I was a little nervous about working as a freelance subcontractor. I'd never done this in the past, before or since my stroke, and had never really been interested in working on my own. I knew that I had the discipline to plan my day and accomplish my daily goals. But I was afraid of feeling lonely. I'm a "people" person, I like being around other people. So, every day I planned to do something that would get me out of the house: chores, shopping, going out for lunch and if I could arrange it, meeting friends. I continued to attend the Toastmasters club and the monthly meetings of the local chapter of the retired government workers.

Every morning, I got up early with Stephanie, exercised, showered, shaved and dressed, ate breakfast and read the newspaper. At nine a.m. sharp (at the end of my favorite morning talk show), I started work.

My first project was a three dimensional model of a pill container—one of those plastic boxes that has a compartment for each day of the week. I stood it up on one end, and opened the Sunday cover so you could see inside one compartment.

My new 35 mm camera was loaded with high-speed film so I wouldn't need a flash. We were instructed not to use a flash since it would distort the color. They suggested using outdoor lighting, since it provided the widest spectrum. I carefully carried all of my equipment outside, one item at a time so I wouldn't drop anything, and set it up on the patio.

I put the camera onto the tripod, focused on the pill box, set the lens according to specifications, and took my pictures. The pill box was on a turntable, so I could keep the camera settings, and just turn the pill box to get it from every angle. Using only one hand, it took me all morning to do this. With so many steps to follow, I didn't notice how fast the time went by. Before I knew it, it was noon. I stopped to watch the news and have lunch.

After lunch, I took the film to a one-hour developer. The first roll came out too dark, so I had to redo it the next morning. Our instructor had warned that the most trouble with this business wasn't with the software, but with the photography: taking quality photos to start the project.

After a few tries, I was ready to have the photos scanned onto a CD-ROM. Since I needed a high quality scan, they had to be sent out. While I was waiting, I photographed my next project: a box of dental floss. I had bid a few hundred dollars for both the pill box and floss box, and my bids had been accepted. I thought I could whip these out in a few weeks as part of my learning curve, then move on to the projects I really wanted to do: the model train cars. One afternoon, I went with one of my model train friends to scout for models. This was too much fun to be work!

When the store called to say my scanned pictures were ready, I was so excited to get started, I was happier than I'd felt in a very long time. I was my own boss, and starting an interesting and creative new business.

I loaded the scanned photos into the computer graphics program, and started. The program displayed two views of the pill box, and gave me a screen to record the outlines. Then it calculated a three dimensional model. The first one was so far off it was funny. There wasn't one straight line or 90 degree angle. But the program was built to fix this.

I knew that each point had to be nudged along the x, y or z axis to form a straight line. This was painstaking and time-consuming work. Periodically, I'd check the display, to see the model of the pill box looking more and more square. It was a nice feeling.

I was good at concentrating, and also a little too good at keeping my energy levels high by raiding the kitchen. Even so, it seemed to take forever to get all the points to line up straight. I printed out copy after copy of the pill box coordinates, until they looked right. Then, I went on to the next view. Each object needed three or four views for the program to generate a complete three-dimensional model.

I checked the company's bulletin board from time to time to see what models and progress the other subcontractors were making. Some people seemed to be able to get things out a lot faster. When I called the technical help desk, they suggested that I go back to the presenter who signed me up.

He looked at my disk and my photos, and gave me a number of good ideas. Then he told me to start the project over from scratch. I was a little frustrated by that, but Stephanie reminded me that in any new job, you have a learning curve, and you always learn from your mistakes.

So, I started over. I was hoping that as soon as I delivered my first two little projects, I could get into the real moneymaker and the fun: train models. I was trying not to think about the fact that two months had gone by and I hadn't earned a dime yet. The promise was there, so I kept going.

Finally, I finished my first project. I logged onto the company's computer "bulletin board" and followed the instructions to send the electronic files that contained my model. After twenty minutes, and only half-way through the transmission, the bulletin board disconnected me. I had to start over. I was disconnected again, and again. When Stephanie came home from work, we tried again. Now, my home business was taking up much more than eight hours a day, moving into our quiet evening time. Stephanie was nice about it, since she wanted me to succeed. We knew that once I'd learned the process, I'd be able do this by myself.

As a back-up, I sent my photos, print-outs and disk by regular mail as well. The contract said they would respond within a few days. After about a week I called. They said that they'd received my back-up materials in the mail, but never received the files I sent through the bulletin board. This made me mad, but the technician said that he'd review my work and get back to me.

So I continued on my other project, a box of dental floss, and checked my bulletin board mailbox. A few days later, the technician sent me a file. I was so excited, I printed it out right away. He complimented me on the very accurate wireframe, the structure underlying the computer model. This made me feel good, my geometry skills had paid off. Then he said that the quality of the photographs were not good enough to generate a clear model, and pointed out places that were blurry or shadowy.

He said that I'd have to start over again. I couldn't believe it! I called him to see if I could just send new photos. I had spent more than two months on this project, and didn't want to have to start over.

"I'm sorry," he said, "but the model just isn't clear enough to pass our quality test. We can't pay for models that don't meet standards. Maybe you should ask your instructor for a little more advice on taking pictures."

That's when I found out that my presenter had left the company, and they hadn't found a replacement in my area. I decided to cut my losses on the pill box project, finish the floss box, and put in a bid for the train model. My bid for the train was accepted. It would mean more time and more work, but also a lot more money. I'd just have to be more careful with the photography.

To break up my at-home work day, I kept my other interests and hobbies going. One of my favorites subjects is the space program. I had received notice of a meeting downtown for a small citizens group that was interested in promoting "cheap access to space," using a new type of rocket that worked more like an airplane. I thought that this was a great idea. Someday I might be able to visit my brother in Hawaii by taking one of these rockets—single-stage-to-orbit reusable vehicles (the one I liked was the X-33 prototype)—and get there in only three hours. I called the group's organizer and told him to count me in. I put on a suit and tie and joined them for their three-day "March Storm," where fifty everyday people met to hear about new space programs, and visit Congressmen's offices to lobby for funding.

I was teamed with two other volunteers. Although the others did most of the talking, I was able to say a few words, and even with my aphasia, make a strong point to support these programs. Maybe it was my disability that made the Congressional staffers take notice. After all, here was a stroke survivor with his own problems, lobbying for the space program. I had a great time, and enjoyed meeting others who shared my interests.

A month later, one of the attendees described the program in an article for the organization's journal, and included a note about me. I was touched by what he wrote:

Despite his difficulties in movement and communications caused by a stroke, one of our team members, Paul Berger, was a strong asset to our team's effectiveness. Because he listened intently to what the staffers were saying, he was able to pick up on and respond to important issues, which won over the staffers.

I also attended several dinners throughout the year, informal briefings for a group of a dozen local activists, at a Chinese restaurant near Capitol Hill. This was a "cause" I believed in very strongly, not only for my own interest in one day being a passenger, but because I thought that U.S. businesses should develop this technology and make travel available to the world. I'm looking forward to the day that the rocket will complete its test phase and go into production.

Throwing myself deeply into an interest that was so far removed from my daily life was one of the best ways I'd found to conquer my disability, to cope with my problems, to keep busy and not get depressed. It was a source of mental and emotional stimulation, pushing myself to learn new things and feeling part of a special cause.

179

In some ways, I saw a parallel between the space program and my stroke. I was in the hospital when I watched the Challenger space shuttle blow up on television. While I was struggling to regain my physical and speech abilities, NASA was rebuilding its space program. Now as I watch the X-33 slowly, methodically, develop into a new kind of rocket, I feel that this new rocket will conquer global travel, just as I have conquered my own world of challenges.

The space program wasn't my only interest. One weekend when Stephanie and I were in New York City, I thought it might be nice to visit the headquarters of the National Aphasia Association, an association dedicated to my speech problem. I wanted to get involved, to learn more about my aphasia and to help others learn to cope as I had. We were able to meet the executive director at her office. We talked for about two hours, and she invited us to come to the next Board meeting, to observe and meet the other Board members.

A few weeks later, we received the agenda for the next meeting, and made arrangements to return to New York City. After attending the first meeting, where they discussed developing an Internet website for NAA, I got excited about being involved. I made the point during the meeting to the website developer that it was very important to use easy icons, a simple format, nothing too busy. People with aphasia need things presented in a clear, easy-to-read way. Later, the developer sent us samples to review, and I dictated my comments to Stephanie. She added some of her own, and I faxed it in. We were later invited to join the Board.

Another strategy to break up my day was an afternoon walk around the neighborhood. One day, I met a neighbor who suggested that I attend a stroke survivors support group nearby. I called the group's organizer, and went to their next weekly meeting. After the meeting, they went to a restaurant for lunch and invited me to go with them. This became a weekly Friday ritual that I just couldn't miss.

When I called again about the status of my floss project, a new technician answered. He explained that they were going through a lot of growth, and had hundreds of projects to review and were a little behind. A few days later, when I called again, he admitted that my project had been lost and I should resend it. So I did. A few weeks later, they rejected it too. I was so frustrated that I couldn't concentrate on my train model. Six months had passed since I'd first signed the subcontractor agreement, and I had nothing to show for it except a pile of photo shop receipts and thick files of unappreciated computer graphics.

This was not working for me. It was clearly time for a personal accounting and a new plan.

Choosing My Future
1996

"Paul, they gave you good marks on your computer work, the wireframes," Stephanie said. "Why not start there?"

She was trying to help me find a direction, and reminded me that the company boasted about how its software could produce CAD-like drawings easier than the sophisticated computer-aided drafting software used by engineers and architects.

"The community college offers CAD classes," Stephanie said. "I can call and get more information."

I didn't want to go back to school after eight years of speech therapy, but a two-month computer course would be reasonable. She arranged a meeting with both the CAD instructor and the college's counselor for disabled students. I took samples of my computer work and the graphics software manual to show the instructor what I'd been doing, to see if he thought this would indeed translate into CAD work.

The meeting was not what I had expected. The CAD instructor suggested that taking a single course in CAD software wouldn't be enough for me to find a job.

"Paul, if you don't have training in the basics of drafting," he said, "you won't understand the purpose of the software. We offer one-year programs that lead to drafting certificates in electrical engineering and architecture. I think you should consider taking one."

"We can supply any assistance you need, at no cost," the disabled students' counselor offered. "Someone to take notes, allowance for untimed tests, or extra time to complete assignments. There's also a special class for learning disabled students that explores different occupations and provides moral support while you figure out what you want to do."

"Thanks, but I don't know. I don't know," I said aloud, thinking, "whoa!" I had gone into this meeting with the idea of taking one summer school class, then getting a job. Now they were talking about a one-year certificate program. This would take some soul-searching.

I was intrigued about the idea of architectural drafting, and carefully read the community college's brochures on the course descriptions and the job titles of graduates of their programs. I wanted to see exactly what a drafter did in real life. I asked a few of my friends if they knew any architects who employed drafters that would let me visit.

My friend Alan, a real estate attorney at my former city department, found a young CAD operator. He showed us how he developed blueprints and building plans on the computer with the CAD software, how he scanned in old drawings and updated them, and how easy it was to make professional drawings. He suggested that instead of going to the community college, I should check out the private technical school he had attended. The school had a good reputation, especially in its placement of graduates.

The CAD operator seemed to like his work, and it looked interesting. He said he thought that I could do the work. The CAD instructor at the community college had agreed that I could learn drafting, as long as I learned it on the computer, since I wouldn't be able to do the manual drafting with just one hand.

I was at another turning point. *Did I want to go back to school? Would this credential guarantee me a job, when I had had so much trouble finding work last year? Did I want to go into computer-aided drafting as yet another career direction?* Many years ago, when I first met with the counselors at the Department of Rehabilitative Services, they had asked if I wanted to be retrained for a new occupation. At the time, they had suggested occupations for which I had absolutely no interest. I turned them down then. *Was I now ready to be retrained?*

I tried to think about the pros and cons of CAD work. I liked the feeling of building things, the concreteness of seeing a structure go up. I was good with geometry and good with modeling. The aphasia had prevented me from being able to speak or write at a professional level, so my options were very limited. The accounting and clerical work I had done since my stroke was boring; I didn't want to go back to it. The CAD work looked fun; it looked like something I would like to do. Plus, the CAD operator said that his private technical school would help me find a job. That was very appealing. *Did I want to suffer through another year of schooling to find a job? Should I go to the private school or the community college for this training?*

The private drafting school had a branch about twenty minutes from home, about the same distance as the community college. Stephanie called them and set up an appointment for us, so I could get a little more information to help me make a decision. I met with the instructor, and explained some of my limitations. He said that he would love the challenge to help me succeed, and thought that there were many ways to make the adaptations I would need. He agreed that for the more detailed, professional drawings, I'd have to depend on the computer, not manual drafting. That was fine with me, since I was very comfortable with computers.

Then one of the administrators reviewed my tuition options. I wasn't eligible for any of their tuition support programs, so we'd have to pay out of our own pockets for the whole thing, and—not surprisingly—one month at the private school cost as much as one semester at the community college. This would be a big financial sacrifice for us, so now, my decision to return to school was complicated by having to decide if the private school was worth the huge expense.

The big difference was that at the community college I would attend traditional classes and labs. At the private school, they simulated a working environment. Full time students were expected to attend from nine a.m. to two p.m., five days a week, working at your own pace. The instructor would explain each exercise as you were ready for it, then supervise you during the day. I liked that concept; with my aphasia, I needed to be able to go at my slower pace, and to have individual help.

They wanted me to start with the July class, but I needed more time to think this through. I told them that I'd probably start in September.

I used June, July and August to think about my future. Working as a draftsman, I'd be doing something related to my previous career plans in real estate: I'd be drawing blueprints for buildings. It was a skilled professional job, more than just the clerical work I'd been stuck with since my stroke. It would give me a much better self-image.

Before my stroke, I had sketched, designed my train layout and painted scenery with my right hand. Now I needed to prove to myself that I could sketch with my left hand. I practiced all summer. I sat in a restaurant at lunch and sketched tables, chairs, art and wall hangings, salt and pepper shakers, and other items.

Stephanie reminded me that when I was first recovering from my stroke and couldn't write at all, I'd try to draw pictures of what I meant. She said that usually the pictures were just a few strokes on the paper, almost as incomprehensible as my speech. She was happy to see how realistic the objects looked now; that I had drawn them to look three dimensional.

Because I didn't have much else to do, I attended the community college's learning disabled support group and job search classes. It was fun; we made field trips to see various occupations in action: to the airport to meet airport security workers and the attendants who pushed travelers needing wheelchairs; to the National Cathedral's hothouse where volunteers helped grow herbs. I learned about occupations I'd never known existed. I had always loved learning new things. Just being on the community college campus during the summer made me feel young and alive. Most of all, I became more and more convinced that computer drafting would be a good match for my interests and skills.

Although Stephanie was very upset about the huge financial commitment for the private drafting school, she agreed that it would be a much more appropriate setting for me. And, the CAD operator I met had said that the school was excellent at placing their students in good jobs, which she agreed was very important.

185

Finally, I was comfortable with the decision. In some ways, I had never admitted to myself that I wouldn't be able to return to my pre-stroke professional position. I'd never wanted to admit defeat, and I think I tried to blame others for not seeing how intelligent I was, and for not being willing to work with me and work around my language problems.

Despite the two separate sessions at the MS Society's job adjustment program, and many conversations with job counselors, I guess the deeper emotional understanding just didn't happen. I was still looking for a job that would lead me back to my former professional level. And even when I went on all those interviews for clerical and low-level accounting jobs, in my heart-of-hearts I knew these jobs were only temporary, and not what I wanted to do with my life.

It took me ten years to be willing to learn a new profession. I don't want to say that I finally gave up, or accepted my disabilities. That sounds like I was defeated. Instead, I focused on my strengths and redirected my goals. I didn't surrender—I conquered the world by an alternate route.

The choice of learning drafting wasn't open to me ten years earlier. It took the drafting industry that long to develop computer software that I could use, and for architectural firms to adopt it. So, it seemed that everything was coming together at the right time. I was giving up one part of my dream: to return to exactly the way I was before my stroke, but at the same time, I was taking on a new dream, a realistic, if somewhat challenging, goal. And this was the type of challenge I knew I could win. I was good at school work, I knew that all I had to do was work hard and complete each assignment. I would put everything into this and show the world that I wasn't just going to graduate and get a job, but that I was going to get excellent grades and get a great job!

We called the private drafting school's enrollment counselor and reviewed some questions I had about attending. He assured me that they would make any necessary accommodations for my disabilities, including giving me extra time to complete the course work. I had wanted to do the combined architectural and engineering program which was slated for one year, and had thought that I'd need an extra month or so. And I needed to hear them tell me that, yes, they would help me find a job. I mailed in my registration fee and the first month's tuition, and prepared myself for another new adventure, another new goal.

The day after Labor Day I drove to school, excited, nervous, and impatient to get started. They gave me a heavy briefcase stocked with a text book, various professional drafting tools, pencils and pens. It was difficult to carry, since it only had a small handle. I used bags with shoulder straps to free up my good hand to hold onto to handrails and open doors. But my school supplies wouldn't fit into the bag I had, so Stephanie bought me an early birthday present—a really nice accountant's case, about the size of a carry-on bag, with lots of pockets and divided sections for all of my books, papers and tools. It had wheels and a long, pull-out handle. Fully loaded, it must have weighed thirty pounds. I'd lug it down the front stairs, wheel it to the car, then somehow with one hand sling onto the back seat. When I got to school, I'd swing it onto the pavement, roll to the front door, then push open the door by backing into it, pulling my case behind me, just barely clearing the door. Occasionally, the staff or another student would see me coming and hold the door for me.

The first day, they assigned me to a drafting table like the other students, most of whom were just out of high school, and at least twenty years younger. Before I could get on the computer, they wanted me to learn some basic drawing and manual drafting concepts, using pencil and paper. I had to sit on a three-legged stool, which was nearly impossible for me since my weak right side always tilted, and my right foot brace wouldn't let me rest on the foot bar. The first few days I was totally distracted by fearing I'd fall off, and by the pain in my right leg and foot which dangled off the stool.

My instructor asked the school administration if it was possible to adjust the table or get me a different table so I could sit in a regular chair. They told him it wasn't possible, so

Stephanie and I went to an art and drafting supply store to buy a more suitable drafting chair with a back for support, a large foot rest, and wheels, so I could push in and out from my table.

I thought I'd need it to be adjustable so I could get into it at a lower height, then raise it up to the drawing table level. The salesman tried to demonstrate, and we had some fun going up and down. The only way I could get it down was to throw my stomach across the seat. Then I could use the pneumatic lever to raise it up. Fortunately, once I got it adjusted to the drawing table level, I could get in and out of it without having to readjust it.

While we were at the drafting supply store, I also bought an electric eraser. My instructor had suggested that it would be easier for my one-handed use, since I couldn't hold the paper and erase by hand. It was a big hit with my fellow students. At first, I let them take turns borrowing it, because it was a nice way to feel friendly and connected with them. But a few seemed to go overboard and were always borrowing it, and got on my nerves. Finally, I just had to say "no." It bothered me to seem so stingy, and to think that the only reason they were being nice to me was to use my stuff.

Also on my instructor's shopping list was a square of burlap, and stick-on "dots." I was wasting a lot of time taking out my measuring and drawing tools, placing them on my tilted drawing table, then before I could use them, they'd slip off onto the floor. I'd pick them up, and they'd slip off again. The burlap prevented them from slipping off every time (although some did drop once in a while). The stick-on "dots" held my drawing paper and instruction sheet in place so I could follow the steps to complete each lesson. I also brought in the weights and clamps I used with my model trains to hold things down. Even so, I needed additional help.

My instructor was very creative. He devised a system that would hold the rulers and straight edges down so I could trace a line across them. He sent home specifications for a square of magnetic sheet metal about the size of a desk blotter. Stephanie found a sheet metal shop a few miles from our home which could cut the metal to my instructor's specs. Then we went to the hardware store and bought flat magnets that were about two inches in diameter and rated at thirty pounds. I didn't know what that meant until I tried to get them off the magnetic sheet metal. I pulled and pried and couldn't get them off. Somehow, with Stephanie's help, we pulled them off. Then she threaded a heavy shoestring through the center of the magnet so I'd have something to grip and pull. It worked, but sometimes I'd pull and pull, and suddenly it would fly off, almost hitting me or another student who was a little too close—a little bit of slapstick humor in my daily routine.

Stephanie had predicted that I'd need some help with the reading assignments, and in the first week I found that I was having trouble putting all the words together. With my aphasia, I had to hear words read aloud, as well as to see them written, to understand the full meaning of a sentence or paragraph. Stephanie worked with me for the first week or so, so she could have a clear picture of exactly what kind of help I needed.

We put an ad in the local newspaper for a "reliable" tutor, at a very low salary. To our amazement, a medical student, who was taking a semester off, answered the ad. He had studied engineering as an undergraduate, and was happy to help me. He told Stephanie that he was very, very reliable. I liked him a lot—he had a great personality, was very alive, and understood my language problems. He would read a paragraph of text to me, then explain anything that I didn't understand.

Unfortunately, he wasn't reliable. Sometimes he'd call and say he'd be late, then never show up. Other times he'd call and tell me he was out of town visiting his girlfriend. Other times he just wouldn't come or call, and when I tried to reach him, his family didn't know where he was. It hurt my feelings that he left me when I needed him, and it even hurt to fire him, but I needed someone I could depend on.

Stephanie called the tutoring company where we had found my previous speech tutor. It cost a little more, but the director promised to find the right match. The first tutor who came seemed too nervous around me, and we didn't "click." When

Stephanie called the director back, she had a little bit of an attitude, but Stephanie was persistent and another tutor was sent out to meet me. This one was worse! Stephanie called back and had a long discussion about exactly who and what I was looking for. The third one was the "charm." Glen had the right mix of patience and pushiness to help me.

He came two or three times a week for an hour and a half session. I'd always feel better after his session. Sometimes I'd be so confused at school about the assignment, even after the instructor explained it, that I'd get anxious and frustrated and not be able to function. Then Glen would read the section to me, explain a few words, and the light would come on in my brain.

Some of the reading assignments were from books, booklets and other materials that weren't to be taken out of the classroom. I tried to puzzle through the readings on my own, but it was too difficult. I asked my instructor if I could take them home. It was very embarrassing, humiliating, to try to explain. I felt like I was begging for yet more special attention. I hated the feeling, but as painful as it was, I had to ask. It was more important to me to do what I had to do to complete the course work and reach my goal.

My instructor was willing to bend the rules for me, luckily, and let me take home the materials over the weekends. Stephanie helped me copy them at the local copy center, so I could underline phrases I didn't understand, make other notes, and take the time I needed during the week to work with Glen.

In those early weeks, no matter how hard I worked, my one-handed pencil drawings only earned a passing grade. Sometimes I was so overwhelmed that I didn't know what to do. I would come home from school and take a nap and try to forget, but I'd feel worse when I woke up. I wasn't a quitter. I knew that I couldn't do manual drafting, and my instructor knew this too. I wanted to prove myself on the computer now.

Before he'd let me on the computer, my instructor said that I'd have to learn to use the professional pen and ink. Drafters' pens have a very special tip that allows them to draw many different thicknesses of lines. The thickness of a line is very important in guiding the construction of the building or equipment. The pens have cartridges which you fill yourself with ink. I remember how messy cartridge pens had been when we used them in grade school.

Now, with just one hand, I had to figure out how to fill a small cartridge with ink from a bottle, then assemble the cartridge and pen tip. My instructor showed me how, and when he saw that I couldn't do it by myself, he helped me. We both ended up covered in ink. Then, when I tried to use the pen, I blobbed and smeared the ink all over the paper and my hand. I was so mad at myself. I was so angry at my stroke. I felt that I was constantly hitting huge brick walls in the way of my progress.

Soon after the "ink" incident, my instructor set me up at a computer work station. At school, they were using the DOS version of AutoCAD software. This is a technical way of saying that they had an older, and somewhat more difficult-to-use version of the computer drafting software. I tried to follow the instructions on my own, and the instructor spent a some time with me. DOS requires typing and recognizing written commands, many of which were very difficult for me to translate through my aphasia. It didn't take my instructor long to understand my problem.

"Paul," he said sympathetically, "I think you'd do a lot better with the Windows version, since it uses icons—pictures— for all the commands, and you'd be able to just click on them with the mouse instead of having to type in words. The Administration told me that we'll have the Windows version in a few days. Why don't you wait till then to get started."

Somehow, Stephanie was able to locate a student version of AutoCAD for Windows, and install it on our home computer. So, while I was waiting for the school to get the new software, I was able to introduce myself to it at home, with Glen's help. Together, we worked through a half-dozen of the beginning lessons.

Once the Windows version of AutoCAD was installed at

school, I started to complete all of my drawing assignments on the computer. My drawings were almost perfect, thanks to the computer compensating for my having only one hand, and I started to see my grades go up. Now I was averaging A's and B's on all my projects. This made me feel good. This was the student Paul Berger had been, so many years before my stroke.

Getting a good grade on a challenging project was important motivation, since even on the computer, it took me longer to complete assignments than the other students. My aphasic brain just processed information slower, and it was hard work for me. I had signed up for the combined engineering and architectural program, which required four quarters of six courses each. Each course contained six to eight drawing projects, plus reading and written quizzes. By the Christmas break, which was four months, or more than one quarter into the school year, I had only completed three of the first six courses. I was worried about my progress.

At the end of each month, I received a "report card," from my instructor, with my attendance record for the month ("excellent," since I never missed one day for illness), my grade average, which improved with the computer work, and drawing progress, which from the choices of "ahead," "satisfactory," and "behind," was always "behind." My instructor said he wasn't worried. I had jumped ahead in the curriculum to start on the computer; I'd catch up as I became more confident on the computer.

Another New Years Eve came with so much hope. I was pursuing a new goal with a clear view of my future. I felt strong and in control of my life. The first week of January, Stephanie and I celebrated our fifteenth wedding anniversary. It was hard to believe that we'd been married that long, the time seemed to pass so quickly. We decided to have a "virtual" anniversary party, and sent all our friends announcements with a letter telling about the past year. We enclosed a gift coupon to an ice cream store, and encouraged them to make a contribution to our favorite "cause," the National Aphasia Association.

Taking A Different Road to Success
1997-1998

Three months later, by March, it seemed that time was standing still. I was struggling with the school work, far behind where I should have been. Instead of being able to complete two or three drawings per week as most of the other students did, it took me more than a week to complete one. Stephanie and I talked about my options: she said that the Americans with Disabilities Act required schools to give disabled students like me more time to complete course work. But I was feeling overwhelmed, like I'd never finish in this lifetime. I was depressed because no matter how hard I worked, no matter how many extra hours I asked Glen to spend tutoring me, I wasn't getting anywhere. I was afraid that I was going to fail. This was too important to me. The pressure I put on myself was unbearable.

One option was to cut back the curriculum requirements by limiting my goal to an architectural certificate, rather than the combined program I had originally signed up for. Some of the students had said that the reading assignments for engineering were harder, and I wasn't really interested in designing machine parts or drafting circuits. Even though it might give me more options in looking for a job, I was much more interested in architectural drafting. So, I asked my instructor if I could drop back to architectural drafting alone. He agreed, and cleared it with the Administration.

My daily routine was really tough. I would get up early with Stephanie, exercise, shower, dress, have breakfast, then lug my rolling case to the car, and drive about twenty minutes through rush hour to school. I'd be the first one there, often arriving before the teacher. I'd go to the cafeteria in the next building for a cup of coffee, which I had to finish and discard before nine a.m., according to school rules. I worked all morning. At eleven thirty, everyone had to leave for a half-hour lunch. I brought my lunch four days a week, treating myself to the cafeteria food on Wednesdays—one small pleasure to look

193

forward to. It hurt my feelings that none of the other students would sit with me at lunch. Intellectually, I knew that there was a big age difference, but emotionally, I felt that we were all in this together, and I would have liked to get to know some of them.

After lunch, I'd work past the end of the two p.m. school day, usually until three, when the instructor would leave. At first, I'd come home and take a nap for an hour or so, but I found myself just as tired and stressed when I woke up. Coffee, soda and snacks didn't seem to revive me, making it harder to concentrate during my early-evening tutoring sessions. It was a little puzzling to me—sitting all day and feeling tired from sitting, then not feeling any better after a nap. Finally, I discovered that taking a walk around the neighborhood for half-an-hour when I came home from school cleared my thoughts, and made me feel energized and ready to plow into homework.

As the drawing assignments became more and more complex, I noticed that the school's staff didn't have the advanced training to help me take full advantage of AutoCAD. The other students were completing this work manually. And while Glen was able to help me follow the lessons to learn the basics, I realized that I needed more. Stephanie took her typical approach to finding solutions for me: She looked in the newspaper's business section, in the consultant's ads. There she found an engineer, Dave, who consulted in AutoCAD. She called him and asked if he would be willing to come to our house to discuss the possibility of tutoring me.

We made an appointment. That night was the turning point in my schooling. Dave was very patient with me, and the chemistry "clicked" between us. He was impressed with how much I'd already learned and told me so. That was a big, and much needed boost to my confidence. For the first few sessions, I had lists of problems I'd encountered at school. He showed me how to solve each one. Then, he showed me tricks the professionals used to develop perfect drawings.

The sessions with Dave were hard. He gave me a lot of information, and even though he wrote it down, showed me how to do it, then had me try it a few times, after he'd leave, I'd get confused and not be able to do the steps. So we'd start the next session with a review, and after a few more times, I'd get it.

My routine was disturbed in April, when my instructor left for another job. The new instructor was very different—very strict about following the rules. Where the old instructor had seen helping me as a positive challenge of his own, the new instructor had no such interest. He wasn't aware that the old instructor had let me take home the reading selections, and he didn't think he could bend the rules. One evening I had to cancel my session with Glen because I wasn't allowed to bring home the reading materials.

Stephanie downloaded pages of regulations on accommodating handicapped students under the ADA from the Justice Department's website, and sent them into school, with a strongly worded note. It made me feel so bad to have to re-live this humiliation. My self-esteem was the size of an ant. To make matters worse, the new instructor asked me some uncomfortable questions about my tutors. He wanted to know how much I paid them, which I never answered. I thought this was rude and uncalled for. And even though I tried to ignore it, he asked me this two more times. Then, he started to ask when I thought I'd finish my course work. I already felt terrible, I knew I was slow, and far behind where I should be, but why did he have to keep asking me this?

His questions put me under impossible pressure. I couldn't work any harder. I already worked the maximum hours in the classroom, then took my projects home and continued working on them. And almost every night either Glen or Dave tutored me for one or two hours. It was humanly impossible for me or anyone to do more, yet I was still making such slow progress. I didn't know what to say to the new instructor.

Stephanie tried to be supportive and tried to cheer me up by reminding me that in the race between the turtle and the hare, the turtle was slower, but because he kept plodding along, he won in the end.

Finally, I asked my instructor why he wanted to know when I thought I'd finish. He said that the administrator had asked him, and made some suggestion that if I didn't finish by a certain time, there was some government regulation that would penalize the school. I was mad, but Stephanie seemed madder! She downloaded more information on the ADA, and we drafted a very strong memo—which we never sent.

In August, my one year agreement with the school was up, and I estimated I'd need at least another four to six months to finish. Stephanie wrote a letter to the school administrator, saying that I wanted to extend my enrollment and that I was committed to finish. She added that I appreciated the school's accommodations and looked forward to continuing until I completed the course work.

A funny thing happened. Just as I'd set my sights on finishing by January, somehow I was able to complete the assignments faster and faster. I was getting good on the computer, and it was finally making a difference. On my end-of-the-month "report card," my new instructor wrote with exclamation marks, "you've made up 80 hours!!"

From time to time, I tried to help my fellow students who had questions about AutoCAD. I knew tricks that the new instructor didn't know. I knew how to help them. But when I tried, they pushed me away. I don't know why. Was it because of my age, or my disability? Did my impaired speech make them think I didn't know anything? It hurt my feelings when I knew I could help. After all, other students had helped me occasionally, so why was I turned away when it was my turn to help?

Again and again, I would take the hurt, take the pressure, let it bounce of my turtle's shell, and focus straight ahead to my own goal, to finish school and get a good job as a computer drafter. I knew if I worked hard, I'd overcome the limitations of my stroke and achieve my goal. I wanted to prove that I could have a rewarding career.

By my birthday in late September, I could see the end of my course work in just a few weeks! Not only was I whizzing through my assignments, but my walking had improved so much that I could walk more than a mile in only twenty-five minutes. At the beginning of the summer, walking the same distance had taken over an hour.

As I was finishing school, I asked Dave to help me develop my portfolio of drawings. I thought I'd have to print them out full-size and buy a large, expensive portfolio bag like the other students to take to interviews. Instead, Dave convinced me that I could just print out my work samples from my home computer on regular paper. I put them in a regular-sized notebook, organized by topic, with my resume, reference letters and other material included. This was so much easier for me to manage with one hand! Dave also helped Stephanie draft my resume, picking out the right technical terms to use in describing the professional aspects of AutoCAD he'd taught me.

"Are you sad to be finishing and leaving school," Stephanie asked. "You've spent every weekday there for more than a year."

"No, no, no," I answered. Absolutely not. I was happy to be leaving; I had had enough. It was time to move on, to find a good job. I usually enjoyed celebrating events like graduations, but this time I didn't even care. I was thinking about my job search, and nervous about interviewing. The memories of my experience two years ago, seventeen interviews and not one offer had left a wound that hadn't healed.

Happily, the school's administration came through with my first three interviews. Even though the jobs weren't right for me, the practice in showing my work samples, and talking with the interviewers was very helpful. It gave me hope and confidence that I would be working soon.

On the weekends, Stephanie clipped ads for architects, designers and computer-aided drafters for me to send a form letter with my resume, asking if they had any entry level jobs. I also sent a series of letters to architectural firms listed in a Washington area resource book. And I called and dropped off resumes to all my friends and contacts in the business community.

Two very long weeks went by without even one phone call, and no interviews. I was starting to feel nervous. Why did all the other students get jobs but me? When was it going to be my turn? Then, I got three calls the same day, for three more interviews. Two of the jobs seemed really interesting. One was with an architect who designed health centers and HMOs. I had worked on an HMO building just before my stroke, and when I showed the letter of appreciation from the company's manager to the architect who interviewed me, he said that he knew her. As soon as I got home, I called and asked her to call him for me, which she did. I thought this would be the perfect job. Specializing in health facilities was obviously a growing niche, and it matched all of my personal and professional interests.

But there wasn't the same chemistry with the architect as I felt with the civil engineers who interviewed me the next morning. My interview lasted more than an hour and a half, and I felt relaxed. The engineers had nice personalities, and from the start, Andy, the principal of the firm seemed "sold" on me. During the interview, I met three of the staff, they showed me some of their work, asked me questions about how I would manage the drawing in AutoCAD, showed me around the office and seemed interested in my notebook of drawings. Andy was concerned about my stroke and asked how I'd get along. In my halting speech, I managed to get across the concept that I was tough and if I could conquer my stroke to get to this point, it was proof that I was a hard worker.

I was amazed when Andy said, "Paul, if you get another offer, please call me before you accept it." I was sure that meant he'd offer me a job. It made me feel great, even though my first choice was with the architect.

That afternoon, about three hours later, Stephanie picked up the messages on our answering machine, including Andy's job offer, asking me to call him. She was so excited, she called me at the restaurant where my stroke group met for a late lunch every Friday. Looking forward to spending Friday afternoons with these friends was one of the important supports that helped me get through each week at school. So it was nice to share with them the very moment that I got my new job. I had Andy's number with me, since I was showing his company brochure to the group. I called him back and he said that he was sending me a letter, and would send it overnight if I wanted. I said, "yes." Since I hadn't heard from the architect, I'd take this job. I told him that I'd sign the letter-of-agreement and return it on Monday. It was the Monday before Thanksgiving, and I'd agreed to start the following Monday, the first of December.

Over the weekend, I thought about everything leading up to this new job. I wished that I could've shown the evaluators at the Department of Rehabilitative Services how wrong they had been when they said I'd never work! Maybe I should thank them, because their negative attitude played a part in motivating me to get to this point.

Starting a new job for anyone is a stressful experience. For me, a forty-eight-year-old, starting in an entry-level position, beginning a new career, overcoming a stroke, it was stressful. But I remember fighting tears of happiness as I was learning new things about civil engineering. It felt so right, I was overwhelmed with emotion. My nerves showed up in a strange popping noise in my jaw when I chewed. Although this cleared up in about a week, from time to time my jaw hurt.

That holiday season was sweet. I was proud to go to Stephanie's company's Christmas party, now with a new identity—CAD operator. But I felt like royalty when Stephanie came to my company's party.

For a few days between Christmas and New Years, we went down to Florida to visit my parents. It was wonderful to share my success with my family, take a few days in the sun, and recharge for the excitement that the New Year in my new career would bring.

But no situation is perfect. I was really slow and having a hard time for the first few weeks. They used the DOS version of AutoCAD, which required a lot of typing. I had learned the Windows version and was much faster recognizing icons and drawing with mouse clicks. I spent a lot of time trying to learn this older version. The other CAD operators were nice to me, and the engineers seemed patient, and I worked as hard as I could to be a productive part of the team. I knew I'd be nervous until the three months' probationary period was up. I wanted this to work more than anything I can ever remember.

Andy said that they were planning to upgrade AutoCAD soon, and I was really surprised one morning when I found it installed on my computer. It was the very latest version, two years improved over the Windows version I'd used at home and school. It was so improved that I didn't recognize some of the icons. I was angry that they hadn't told me exactly when this was coming, and frustrated that they didn't offer any instruction. It ruined my day. Finally, I told my supervisor, Jim that I couldn't get any work done. He showed me how to switch back to the old DOS version, and I managed to do a little.

The next morning, Andy passed me in the hall, and said enthusiastically, "How's the new software? You must be clicking away like an expert!"

"No, it's bad," I said, too frustrated to bring up any other words. I didn't realize that that was the wrong thing to say to him, until later that week.

The most constant force in my life since my stroke had been the roller-coaster ups and downs. And I was so high with this new job, it was time to come down. I just wished it hadn't been such a fast, deep plunge. That Friday, in mid-January, six weeks after I'd started with the civil engineers, at the end of the day, the two senior partners, Andy and Bill, and my supervisor, Jim, called me into the conference room, then closed the door. I knew something was wrong when they did that. Andy gave me the bad news—I was fired. He said that I was too slow and took up too much of my co-workers' time asking questions. He said that I talked too much. *Imagine me, with my aphasia, for whom getting out a few words was a real accomplishment, was being accused of talking too much!* He said that they were too busy and too small a company to keep me. They needed someone who worked faster.

I was really shocked because no one had said anything

about this during the past six weeks. They had complimented my work. I had just asked Bill on Monday if I could work overtime, and he had said, yes, that there was plenty of work to do. And on Thursday, he had asked everyone to work over the weekend. I was looking forward to a whole extra day of overtime, and to the nice feeling of being part of a team.

I tried to keep my wits, and hoped some words would come through my aphasic mouth. I said that I was a hard worker, and it wasn't my fault. I was fast in AutoCAD for Windows, and had to spend time learning DOS, which was a lot slower to use anyway. I said that none of the other employees knew Windows either, so it wasn't fair. I knew that I was slow, but I'd get faster, just like I did after a few months at school.

Earlier in the day, I had tried to tell Bill how much better I was on the new software now, but he was on the phone. I wished that they had given me a few more weeks to prove myself. They said that they'd ask some other companies if they had openings. I asked them to give me a week or two to keep working while I looked for a job, but Andy said, "no."

I went back to my cubical, and wrote up my hours for the week. I tried to call Stephanie to tell her, but she didn't answer her phone. Then, I packed up all of my stuff—coffee mug, snacks, books, notes, and one of the other CAD operators helped me put my chair in the car—I had brought it in earlier that week so I could work at the drafting table.

I said "goodbye" to the others. They were surprised that I had been fired. I had just had lunch with them that day and we talked about everything.

I drove home, still shocked, and very sad. I thought about what a good job it was. I had learned a lot about civil engineering, and realized how much I really liked it, designing commercial buildings and the areas around them. The job had great benefits: good pay, pay for overtime, a promise of a pension fund, and a "cafeteria" health plan. And I enjoyed being part of a team. I thought that I'd have the opportunity to move up their ladder, from CAD one, to two, to three, to Engineering Technician. I had wanted to be part of this company for many years.

Earlier that week, I had thought about nominating them for an "Employer of the Year" award, given by my county's disability organization. I was feeling so good about them that the disappointment of losing this job really cut to the core.

I wanted to scream, I wanted to cry, I wanted to hit someone or something. But I don't do those things when I'm frustrated or beaten. I do my thing: analyze the situation. I wanted to understand why this had happened to me. Why was God tormenting me? Why couldn't I just do what "normal" people do—go to school, get a job, keep a job? And I was thinking, what if Andy or Bill had had a stroke. Would they have had the energy, the determination, the courage to overcome all this disappointment and do all the hard things it takes to get through a day dragging around a stroked-out body?

Now I had to start over again. Stephanie helped a little by pointing out the positive side of this: that I'd learned I liked civil engineering; I could work a full day, plus overtime; make a long drive through rush hour traffic; and have the energy to exercise on the bike at home. They'd taught me some new things, and I was a little faster on AutoCAD. Hopefully this would translate to a better start at my next job, and so a better chance of keeping it.

I followed up on two phone calls I'd received from resumes sent out in November. My tutor, Glen, had called the week before to tell me about a friend who was looking for CAD operators. I took my resume to his house, and showed him my work. He was supportive, and made me feel good. The drafting school's administrator didn't blink an eye. He said to list my six weeks with the civil engineering firm on my resume, then went to work to get me more interviews. I sent out resumes, had a few interviews, then received a call from Ken.

Ken needed an entry-level CAD operator, but had some questions about my resume. "You've done a little of everything," he said, "so tell me why you want an entry level job now."

I hesitated for a minute, but I had to be honest. "I have a

202

stroke," I answered. "My speech...not good. My drafting... good."

"Okay," Ken said. "Can you come tomorrow and show me what you can do? At ten?"

"Yes!" *He wanted me even with my stroke.* That made me feel great.

"We're on the second floor, and there's no elevator," he said. "Will that be a problem?"

"Is there a hand...hand...handrail," I said, finally getting the word out.

"Handrail? Yes."

"No problem," I said. He gave me directions, which I listened to politely, but couldn't take down. It's just something I can't do with my aphasia. I had his phone number on caller ID, and his address from the ad. I'd use the computer yellow pages to find his office and print a map of his exact location.

"See you tomorrow, Paul," Ken said.

"Yes, thank you."

The next day I put on my best interviewing tie and jacket, and arrived early. I had a good feeling about this. Ken was the president of a small company. They did contract work preparing blueprints for the systems inside buildings—plumbing, heating, electrical. The work sounded great.

We met in his office, which he shared with another engineer. Then he showed me into the next room. It was a large open space, with desks for three engineers on one side and work stations for four CAD operators in the middle. Ken introduced me to the others. All of them seemed nice. He asked me to sit at one of the computers and show him that I could find my way around AutoCAD. Thankfully, they were using AutoCAD for Windows, a version I could use easily.

"We're really backed up," Ken said. "You can start today if you're free."

I couldn't believe what I'd heard. He wanted me to start right away. I wasn't ready for that. It was Thursday, I had errands to run, grocery shopping, and I didn't want to miss my Friday lunch with the stroke group.

"Monday?" I asked.

"Okay," Ken said.

I asked if I could have an hour in the morning once a month to continue my physical therapy. He agreed. I told him I had plans to go to Chicago for a week in June to attend the meeting of the National Aphasia Association. He agreed. We haggled over the starting salary, then shook hands.

I had a new job.

I danced down the stairs, drove home and called Stephanie. She was so happy for me, too.

I was determined to make this work. I wasn't going to be surprised like I was at the last job. If Ken or the CAD supervisor, Jack, didn't give me feedback to let me know how I was doing, I was going to ask them. This time, I wanted the chance to fix any problems before they got out-of-hand. I knew I could be a good CAD operator, if only they'd give me time to prove myself.

I looked forward to going to work every morning. There was a warm, family feeling in the way the office was set up: open, casual (including wearing casual clothing, which I'd really come to appreciate during my year at school), friendly. It made the day go by quickly.

The office was only a twenty-minute drive from home, which was considered close-by in the Washington metro commuting area, and a lot closer than my previous job with the civil engineers. Most days I ate lunch at my desk, then in the early afternoon, took a half-hour walk to revive. I came back and worked until six or six-thirty, sometimes even later.

At the end of each week for the first month or so, I asked my supervisor, Jack what he thought about my work, and stopped Ken to see if he thought that I was doing okay. They were a little surprised by my questions, and sometimes they told me that I was slow or had this or that problem, but most of the time, they said my work was fine.

After a few months, working an average of fifty hours a week and some Saturdays, I felt more confident and comfortable. They were planning to keep me. This new job was better than my first CAD job. Everything had worked out for the best. I wasn't fast, and some days were better than others, but I had proven that you can get knocked down, then pick yourself up again. I'm proud of what I've done. I'm still a little mad at the people along the way who made it harder for me to achieve my goals, but I'm proof that you don't have to surrender, just take another route to success.

That summer, I attended the National Aphasia Association's meeting, and gave a speech on "How I Cope With Aphasia." Since I knew that standing in front of two hundred people would make me very nervous, I spent months preparing. First, I wrote out the speech, with Stephanie's help. Then, I had a practice run at my Toastmasters club meeting.

I gave the following notes to the Toastmaster of the evening to introduce me:

"Paul wanted me to give you this information as an introduction to his speech," the Toastmaster said. Then she continued with my notes. *"Paul will be presenting this speech during the first national meeting of the National Aphasia Association, "Speaking Out," in Chicago on June 4. Paul will be on a panel with three other speakers, entitled, 'Coping with Aphasia.'*

"Aphasia is the speech disorder Paul has. One million people in the U.S. also have aphasia, and like Paul, most acquire it after suffering a stroke. In one year, as many as 80,000 new cases of aphasia are identified.

"Aphasia is a communication disorder, where the language functions in the brain—speaking, reading and writing—are lost or mixed up. The brain "rewires" itself to compensate and often the result is broken-up speech, like Paul's. Sometimes the wrong word comes out, even though he knows in his mind what he wants to say. And that's why Paul has asked me to hand

205

out a copy of his speech too, so you can read along."

Then I stood at the lectern and gave my speech:

How I cope with aphasia.

It is hard! I keep busy, so I do not get depressed. I have many interests to keep me busy. One interest is the space program. I started when I was a young boy, I remember watching a rocket go to the moon at four in the morning on TV. I made a scrapbook with newspaper clippings of every satellite and rocket. In high school, I joined the space club. We had a real control room and a space capsule. I remember sitting at the controls and making the capsule turn.

My first date with my wife, Stephanie, was at the Air and Space Museum to celebrate the 10th anniversary of Neil Armstrong landing on the moon.

January 1986, I had a stroke. I was in the hospital watching TV when the shuttle exploded.

A few years ago, I went to a meeting of a space club in Washington, D.C. I learned about a new rocket ship, a single-stage-to-orbit rocket, to use over and over like an airplane. I think this rocket is important for the future of the US space program.

In the past 3 years, I went to Congress with the Pro-Space society. I went with 2 other people to talk to the Congressmen. I have aphasia, but I can say some words to help lobby. The Congressmen and staff remember me because I have aphasia and an interest in the space program. I write and phone Congress and the President on new bills.

I learn about space news in many ways:

(1) I go to dinner 2 or 3 times a year with people from Pro-Space.

(2) I read newsletters and magazines.

And (3) I get e-mail and watch different Internet sites.

Learning about space keeps me busy and thinking

about the future, not about my problems.

This is how I cope with aphasia!

During Toastmasters club meetings, it's customary for the people attending to vote for the best speaker of the evening. I'm a competitive person, and I really, really wanted to win. And that evening, I did. I won the "Best Speaker" prize, a miniature lectern and certificate.

I won.

Giving Back
1999-2001

I believe that jury duty is part of an American's civic duty. When the official forms arrived in the mail requiring me to register, I thought a lot about this responsibility. I was concerned that my aphasia would prevent me from participating. Sometimes I needed people to repeat what they said. And, it was hard for me to listen and take notes at the same time. On the form, there was a section on accommodations for people with disabilities. I listed the need for a note-taker, and sent it in. More than a year passed, and I wondered if they had disqualified me because of my aphasia.

Then, the summons came. Unless there was some work or family emergency, the notice instructed me to report for jury duty at the end of the month. As the day drew near, I became anxious, fearing the unknown. This was a new experience that I would have to do on my own. I worried about everything: Where would I park? Would I find the jury room? Would I be able to have a cup of coffee? Would I be able to follow instructions and keep up with the other jurors?

Some of my co-workers tried to make me feel better by describing their experiences. I read the information for jurors posted on the county's website. One night after work, Stephanie and I took a test drive to the court house so I could find my way around. I was still nervous, but I knew I could do it.

The big day arrived. I left early with a bag I had packed the night before: magazines to read, paper to take notes, dried apricots for energy, the juror's parking permit, and official forms.

"This is an adventure," I told myself, trying to stay calm. I drove around the parking lot to the handicapped parking. I walked about a block downhill to the main entrance. Inside, I placed my bag on the security belt and walked through the metal detector.

"Jury?" I asked, showing the guard my summons. He pointed down the hall.

I saw a sign over the juror's waiting room door. I walked in, showed my papers, and signed in. They gave me a card and told me to take a seat and wait. I sat next to a nice woman who was knitting. The man sitting across from me had a cup of coffee.

"Where coffee?" I asked.

"There's a cafeteria around the corner," he answered.

I returned just as they started a video. Seeing and hearing about the process was very helpful. They called the first set of jurors. I listened intently but didn't think they called my name. They called for a second set of jurors, and this time, I heard my name. I left my things and went to the desk with about twenty other people.

"Paul Berger," I said, feeling like a soldier called into action.

My group spent about twenty minutes getting up to the courtroom on the fourth floor, and waiting outside. The door opened, and a clerk told us that the parties had settled, and so didn't need a jury. We were sent back downstairs. This happened again. Called up for action, then dismissed.

The third time, we were ushered into the courtroom. The judge greeted us. Then, the attorneys huddled in front of the judge's bench, whispering to the judge and each other. They sat down, and the judge dismissed us. When we returned to the juror's room, the clerk told us we could go home.

As I was driving to my favorite diner for a late lunch, I thought, *That wasn't so bad!* I didn't actually sit through a trial; maybe next time. Feeling patriotic, I knew that I would not be afraid to do this again.

Thursday after the presidential elections of 2000, when the country did not know whether Bush or Gore was our president, I was having a good day at work. I was still at the same engineering consulting company, drafting blueprints. In the two-and-a-half years since I started, the company had merged with another similar group. I was assigned to the electrical section, to specialize in computer-aided drafting of lighting in commercial buildings. Soon after the merger, the office moved near an industrial park. There were sidewalks on one side of the street, so I could continue to take my afternoon walk.

Being an adventurer, I also walked on the other side of the street where there were no sidewalks. That Thursday, it was a sunny, pleasant November day in the suburbs of Washington, DC, and as I strolled along on the grass, I suddenly caught my right foot in a hole that was covered by leaves. I twisted my ankle and fell hard to the ground, landing on my right shoulder.

I lay there for a few minutes, stunned and hurting. I watched people driving by look at me. But no one stopped to help. Although my good left leg and arm were a little sore, I was able to push myself up and stand on my left leg. I hopped across a four-lane road to take the short cut back to my office.

I took the elevator to the second floor, and hopped down a long corridor to my cubical. My right foot hurt too much to think about work, so I called Stephanie.

"I fell," I told her. "And it hurts."

"Did you break your leg?"

"I don't think so."

"Do you want to go to the hospital?"

"I don't know."

"How bad does it hurt," Stephanie asked.

"I don't know," I answered.

"Well, if you don't know how much it hurts, how can I tell you what to do?" she said, sounding concerned, but a little annoyed. "Why don't you see how you feel and call me back in an hour."

I hung up the phone, and asked Greg and Harry what they thought I should do. A few minutes later, most of the people in my office had gathered around to inspect my injuries, advising me to go to the hospital. I called Stephanie, and told her that I could drive since my left leg was okay, and would meet her at home. Greg and Harry helped me get to my car. By the time I got home, my right ankle was puffed up twice its normal size.

Stephanie helped me into her car and drove to the Emergency Room at the same community hospital where they had taken me 14 years earlier, suffering from a ruptured aneurysm. She parked in the wrong area, so I had to limp around the hospital, now in a lot of pain, to the ER's "express window." This was where the runny noses, cut fingers, and sprained ankles were sent.

The doctor examined me, at first concerned that I had fallen because I had had a second stroke. After she was satisfied that I had just stepped into a hole, I went for x-rays. Nothing was broken. But my ankle and foot were severely sprained, and the doctor told me that I would have to stay off it for a few days. We talked about crutches, but with one hand, they wouldn't work.

I spent Friday, Saturday, and Sunday in bed or on the sofa with my right foot propped up, watching the non-stop cable news on the presidential recount. Between my strong interest in politics and the medication, I was feeling happy.

By Monday, I needed to get back on my feet. About three months earlier, I had started to wear a new kind of lightweight, strap support for my right ankle. Now to protect my sprained foot, I had to return to the old solid plastic brace. I also had to use my cane, which I hadn't used for many years, even to walk around the house.

I was a little depressed by this setback, but couldn't let it get to me. Later that week, I was starting a new adventure. For the first time, I had a booth at the national meeting of the American Speech Language Hearing Association, downtown at Washington's convention center. I was promoting copies of the first edition of the book you are reading now. In a way, writing and speaking about my experiences had become a second, part time job.

Like all convention centers, I had a long walk from the door to my booth. If I walked slowly, and leaned on my cane, it didn't hurt too much. Stephanie helped me set up the booth. I had poster boards with photos, books to sell, flyers to distribute, and a bowl of candy to attract visitors. Stephanie helped me prop up my sprained foot on one of the boxes under the table, then went to work and left me to make my pitch to anyone who walked by.

I was nervous. Although I could give a speech if I practiced, my aphasia still made talking hard, especially with the distracting pain in my foot. I reminded myself that this was a speech therapist's convention. They would make the effort to understand me.

Most of the time during my three days at the convention, I handed flyers to the people who came to my booth. The booth on my left was selling videos to train children with speech problems to enjoy parties, and gave away popcorn. I saw a lot of therapists and ate a lot of popcorn. My speech therapist dropped by to store her hand-outs at my booth, and took me to lunch at the cafeteria.

Sitting all day was a little boring, and my sprained foot felt stiff. So every two hours or so, I would take some flyers in a shoulder bag, and with my cane, limp around to the other booths. I tried not to put too much weight on my sore foot. Meeting other exhibitors took my mind off the pain.

At the end of the meeting, I attended a special celebration, including an award ceremony sponsored by the National Council on Communicative Disorders. As I sat in the audience and watched that year's honorees receive their awards, I remembered the previous year's award ceremony. In 1999, I received their Individual Achievement Award. On stage at the Kennedy Center, I gave an acceptance speech to the 1,000 people attending.

To give the speech, I started weeks earlier. I wrote down my thoughts, and Stephanie helped me with the grammar. I reviewed my Toastmasters book for hints on how to organize the speech, to use gestures, and to fight the nervousness of speaking to so many people. I read the speech a few times aloud, then changed some of the words that I couldn't say. I practiced for hours and hours. Then I had a test run, giving the speech to twenty people at my Toastmasters club meeting two weeks before the ceremony.

My parents came from Florida and brother from Hawaii to attend the celebration. Stephanie and I were asked to come early to go over the arrangements. I wanted to walk on stage to check for handrails up and down the stairs. Since I only have the use of one hand, we decided that one of the assistants would hold the award while I gave my speech, then carry it off stage for me.

The time had come. I walked up the stairs, saw the beautiful glass award, nodded, and took my notecards out of my pocket and put them on the lectern. As I had learned in Toastmasters, I calmed myself by taking a deep breath, and looking out over the audience for a friendly face. The spotlight was so bright that I couldn't see anyone. I didn't know that the room was packed. I started my speech, thanking the Council for the award.

I was going along okay, smooth and confident. Then, my aphasia kicked in, and I got stuck on a word. But my Toastmasters training reminded me to just go on, so after a short pause, I continued. My friends and family later told me that they all held their breath, anxious for me, and cheered when I went on.

I wanted the world to know how people with aphasia feel, and said:

> *Life is hard for me because people can not understand my speech problem. It is discrimination. Ramps are built for wheelchairs, but access for people with speech problems is built by making others understand. It is in the head and the heart. It is a battle for everyone. I am proof that we can win the battle.*

I swung my fist up in the air in victory at the end of the speech, and the audience applauded and cheered loudly.

That night, I met John Glenn, the former Senator and astronaut, one of my heroes. His wife, Annie, has a speech impairment and one of the awards was named in her honor. I sat with them during the award ceremony, and asked for the Senator-astronaut's autograph on my program. Then, Annie asked for my autograph on the copy of my book I had given them.

The evening's Master of Ceremonies was Joe Krebs, a

local NBC television news anchor. When he learned that I was one of the awardees, he came to my house to interview me. I showed him my model trains, and the computer drafting work I was doing. He asked Stephanie some questions, too.

The interview ran on TV the days before and after the award ceremony. Many people called, wrote, or emailed me to say that they were inspired by my story. Knowing that I could help others made me feel that some good had come from my stroke.

Another award-winner that night was the producer for the PBS TV program, Healthweek. The producer asked if she could do a story on me. They followed me around for more than two weeks, at home, in the kitchen, in my model train room, at work, and driving down the street. They took old photos of me before my stroke, and after. They edited in some of the videotaped speech, physical and occupational therapy sessions from years earlier. They filmed the speech I gave to the Department of Transportation, during the agency's celebration of National Handicapped Employment Awareness Month.

I felt that my message was finally getting attention—that after a stroke people can live full lives and follow their dreams.

One of the people who saw me on TV worked for a hospital group in my area. She was starting a pilot project with the local American Heart Association's chapter called Operation Stroke, and asked me and Stephanie if we would co-chair the project's Community Education Committee. Now, I would be able to help many people learn the warning signs of stroke, to call 911, and get to the hospital immediately.

I had never been chair of a committee before, and was nervous. I didn't want my aphasia to prevent me from being the best chairman. I thought, *This is just like other big projects I've tackled.* So, we started by setting goals, and making a list of things to do to reach the goals. The staff helped with everything.

The first task was to recruit a committee. I asked my speech and physical therapists, my co-workers, and friends. Stephanie and I were active in local politics, and I was friendly with my Supervisor on the county's Board of Supervisors. She also agreed to be a member of the committee.

The committee members shared my positive, can-do attitude and worked hard. Before each meeting, Stephanie and I talked to the staff to plan the agenda, what we wanted to achieve, and what we thought the next activity would be. As chair, I started the meeting, asked for approval of the minutes, and kept us on schedule. It wasn't easy with my limited speech, but my gestures helped. This built my self-confidence and self-esteem, especially when one of the committee members complimented me on my leadership.

For the first six months, the committee planned creative ways to educate the community by thinking of groups that would reach the most people in the county. We would put posters and cards and bookmarks in libraries and public recreation centers, and have speakers give a slide presentation to groups of retired workers, churches and senior centers.

The program was officially launched to the public during Stroke Awareness Month in May with a stroke screening program at a large fire station. Local politicians and community leaders attended. I gave a speech, along with the neurologist and emergency room physician who headed Operation Stroke. I was interviewed by the county newspaper. This meant that many people would learn that strokes can happen to anyone at any age, so everyone needed to recognize the warning signs.

I was lucky to be at the gym when my aneurysm ruptured, because the staff was trained to call an ambulance immediately. If I had been at home, lifting heavy groceries instead, I probably would have died. I didn't know that a sudden, very bad headache was serious. I didn't think that a 36-year-old could have a stroke, or even how to recognize the symptoms of a stroke. I knew about heart attacks, thanks to the public education efforts of the American Heart Association—I was at the gym exercising to prevent heart disease. Now, this group is dedicated to the same public education for stroke.

After a year of numerous talks by committee members and

boxes of material distributed, the staff had tracked 400,000 contacts. A survey showed significant increases in understanding by people in the county about what to do if you see the symptoms of a stroke.

I think everyone should volunteer for a good cause, because you can make a difference. I know volunteering for Operation Stroke gave me a way to feel creative, to be part of a team, to be a leader, to help something important happen, and to give back.

While I was sitting at my booth at the national speech therapy meeting, I met a therapist who was planning the Ohio Speech Therapy Association's annual meeting. We talked a little, and she took my hand-outs. A few weeks later, she called to ask if I would be available to give the keynote address during her group's award luncheon that Spring. She had a special request—since the meeting was hours of coursework for the therapists, they would appreciate a light-hearted luncheon speech.

Laughing at the funny things about having a stroke wasn't hard, but being able to deliver a humorous speech with fluency, timing, and funny gestures to make others laugh was a big challenge for a person with my severe aphasia. All of the speeches I had presented up to now had been serious and inspirational. I knew that I would have to select the funny stories carefully, and practice many hours to memorize the words and to get the body language right.

One of my favorite funny stories is typical for people with aphasia. Once a week, I go out to lunch at the local deli, and order a sandwich, either turkey or tuna. My aphasia causes me to switch words that are close in sound and meaning. So when I'm thinking that I'm ordering a turkey sandwich, sometimes the word tuna comes out instead. And I don't always catch my mistake, until the sandwich arrives. I like both, and I don't mind the surprise.

The turkey-tuna problem was included in my Ohio speech, along with five other humorous incidents resulting from my aphasia. Because I was worried that people wouldn't laugh, I hammed it up a little in the middle by asking to the audience to laugh, emphasized with a funny gesture.

Stephanie and I arrived in Cleveland the night before the luncheon. This allowed me to have a good night's sleep and an unhurried morning. I checked out the room—how to get on stage, how the lectern was arranged, where to put my cards and glass of water. Unlike the Kennedy Center, where the room was dark and the spotlight prevented me from seeing the thousand people in the audience, this room was set for lunch, the lights were up, and I would be able to make eye contact with most of the 400 therapists watching me.

I was nervous. My speech was at the end of the awards, giving me plenty of time to feel more nervous. To make matters worse, the audio system was on the fritz, and most of the award presentations were shouted out without the assistance of a microphone. I knew the hotel staff were trying to get it fixed.

Unlike most people, I cannot shout. My aphasia limits my range of volume. More than half an hour passed, and the system was still down. It would crackle on, then off again. My nerves were shot. I was afraid that I would not be able to give the speech I had worked so hard to do.

Miraculously, just as the President was about to introduce me, the microphones came back. As I stood, I felt stiff. I walked slowly to the mike, and looked around. I put my note cards on the lectern, and asked for a glass of water. I took a deep breath, and remembered to smile.

I started. As I warmed up, I relaxed a little. I told my stories, and the audience laughed in the right places. I made eye contact and laughed along with them. When I finished, they laughed and applauded. Having a sense of humor is important, as much for therapists, as for stroke survivors and families.

Laughter conquers the world!

Epilogue

Like all Americans, I was deeply moved by the terrorist attacks on September 11. Our lives will never be the same again. The things we took for granted have changed forever. We appreciate our family and friends more. In some ways, these terrible events may help others understand how a stroke survivor's life changes. After a stroke, you can't move around like you used to; often, you lose your job; travel, recreation, money, security, everything changes after a stroke.

And, like America's response to September 11, you can't let the terrorists—or your stroke—keep you from living a full life. For me, I tried to focus on my goals. In January, 2002, I presented my tenth speech to my Toastmasters club, earning the certification of "Competent Toast Master."

In February, 2002, I celebrated four years with my current employer, working full time as a computer-aided drafter. In March, I returned for a fifth year with members of ProSpace to lobby Congress on giving private companies more access to the space program. I was able to visit 17 Congressional offices in three days.

I'm also helping to plan the third national meeting of the National Aphasia Association's Speaking Out 2002 conference, to be held in Washington, DC. And I'm working on a commencement speech for the graduates of the University of New Hampshire's Speech Therapy and Occupational Therapy programs. Some of their comments on my story are featured on the front pages of this book.

Useful Resources

Many people have asked me for information. Here are resources we have used or that other stroke survivors and their families have found useful.

First, some facts: Stroke is America's Number Three killer, and a leading cause of serious disability. Coronary heart disease is Number One. That's why it's so important to know the warning signs, and know how to respond quickly and properly if warning signs occur.

The American Stroke Association lists these warning signs of stroke:

1. Sudden numbness or weakness of the face, arm or leg, especially on one side of the body.

2. Sudden confusion, trouble speaking or understanding.

3. Sudden trouble seeing in one or both eyes.

4. Sudden trouble walking, dizziness, loss of balance or coordination.

5. Sudden, severe headache with no known cause.

The American Heart Association lists these warning signs of heart attack:

1. Chest discomfort that lasts more than a few minutes, or that goes away and comes back. It can feel like uncomfortable pressure, squeezing, fullness or pain.

2. Discomfort in other areas of the upper body. Symptoms can include pain or discomfort in one or both arms, the back, neck, jaw or stomach.

3. Shortness of breath. This feeling often comes along with chest discomfort. But it can occur before the chest discomfort.

4. Other signs: These may include breaking out in a cold sweat, nausea or lightheadedness.

If you have any of these warning signs of stroke or heart attack, call for help immediately. Call 9-1-1 to get an ambulance to rush you to the hospital.

Calling 9-1-1 is almost always the fastest way to get life-saving treatment. Emergency medical services staff can begin treatment when they arrive, up to an hour sooner than if someone gets to the hospital by car. The staff are also trained to revive someone whose heart has stopped. You'll also get treated faster in the hospital if you come by ambulance. Getting help fast for a stroke can mean saving a life and reducing disability. ˙

National organizations which provide helpful information:

American Stroke Association
A Division of the
American Heart Association
7272 Greenville Ave.
Dallas, Texas 75231
For stroke information, call 1-888-4-STROKE
or 1-888-478-7653
For heart information, call 214-373-6300
or 800-242-8721
www.americanheart.org

National Aphasia Association
29 John St., Suite 1103
New York, NY 10038
1-800-922-4622
www.aphasia.org

National Stroke Association
9707 E. Easter Lane
Englewood, Co. 80112
Phone: 303-649-9299
Toll Free: 1-800-STROKES
or 800-787-6537
Fax: 303-649-1328
www.stroke.org

Brain Injury Association
105 North Alfred Street
Alexandria, VA 22314
Phone: 703-236-6000
Family Helpline: 800-444-6443
Fax: 703-236-6001
www.biausa.org

National Easter Seal Society
230 West Monroe Street, Suite 1800
Chicago, IL 60606
Phone: 312-726-6200
Toll free: 800-221-6827
Fax: 312-726-1494
www.easter-seals.org

American Speech Language Hearing Association
10801 Rockville Pike
Rockville, MD 20852
Professionals/Students: 1-800-498-2071
Public: 1-800-638-8255
www.asha.org

American Occupational Therapy Association
4720 Montgomery Lane
P.O. Box 31220
Bethesda, MD 20814-3425.
Phone: 301-652-2682
Fax: 301-652-2682
www.aota.org

American Physical Therapy Association
1111 N. Fairfax Street
Alexandria, VA 22314.
Phone: 800-999-2782
or 703-684-2782
Fax: 703-684-7343
www.apta.org

Neuro-Developmental Treatment Association (NDTA)
1540 S. Coast Hwy, Suite 203
Laguna Beach, CA 92651
Phone: 800-869-9295
Fax: 949-376-3456
www.ndta.org

Family Caregiver Alliance
690 Market Street, Suite 600,
San Francisco, CA 94104.
Phone: 415-434 3388
Fax: 415-434 3508
www.caregiver.org

National Family Caregivers Association
10400 Connecticut Avenue, #500
Kensington, MD 20895-3944
Phone: 800-896-3650
Fax: 301-942-2302
www.nfcacares.org

American Academy of Neurology
1080 Montreal Ave.
St. Paul, MN 55116
Phone: 651-695-1940
www.aan.com.

American Academy of Physical Medicine and Rehabilitation
One IBM Plaza, Suite 2500
Chicago, IL 60611-3604
Phone: 312-464-9700
Fax: 312-464-0227
www.aapmr.org

American Congress of Rehabilitation Medicine
6801 Lake Plaza Drive,
Suite B-205
Indianapolis Indiana 46220
Phone: 317-915-2250
Fax: 317-915-2245
www.acrm.org

Making Progress
Adult Neurological Rehabilitation
Therapy and Consultation
Susan Ryerson, P.T.
5249 Duke Street, Suite 203
Alexandria, Virginia
Phone: 703-370-2970
Fax: 703-370-7209
makingpro@aol.com

Julian Whitaker, M.D.
Nutritional & Complementary Medicine
For the *Health & Healing* newsletter, Dr. Whitaker's books,
and nutritional supplements:
Customer Service
Health & Healing
PO Box 59750
Potomac, MD 20854
Phone: 800-219-8590
www.drwhitaker.com

To visit Dr. Whitaker's clinic:
Whitaker Wellness Institute Medical Clinic, Inc.
4321 Birch St.
Newport Beach, CA 92660
Phone: 800-488-1500
or 949-851-1550
www.whitakerwellness.com

Darlene S. Williamson, MA, CCC-SLP
Speech-Language Pathologist, Therapy and Consulting
11244 Waples Mill Road, Suite G-1
Fairfax, Virginia 22030
Phone: 703-691-3030
Fax: 703-620-1264
Email: dswill50@aol.com

Dog Days Graphics, Marida Hines
Illustrated Design and Marketing Materials
P.O. Box 1353
Washington Grove, MD 20880
Phone: 301-519-8730
Fax: 301-330-2385
dogdaysgraphics@aol.com

Other Websites:

www.strokecenter.org
www.aphasiahope.org
www.thedisabilityresource.com

My Interests and Hobbies:

Toastmasters International
PO Box 9052
Mission Viejo, CA 92690
Phone: 949-858-8255
Fax: 949-858-1207
www.toastmasters.org

National Model Railroad Association
4121 Cromwell Road
Chattanooga, TN 37421
Phone: 423-892-2846
Fax: 423-899-4869
www.nmra.org

ProSpace
www.prospace.org

About the Authors

Paul E. Berger lives with his wife, Stephanie Mensh, and two cats in Falls Church, Virginia, a suburb of Washington, D.C. Paul survived a stroke at the young age of 36. In the years since, he has focused his positive energies on setting goals and following his dreams. Paul was born in Philadelphia, where he graduated with a B.A. from Drexel University. He continued his studies earning an M.A. at the New School in New York City, then an M.B.A. at Marymount University in Arlington, Virginia.

After his stroke, he earned a certificate in Architectural Drafting, and started a new career, working full time for building engineering consultants. Paul based *How to Conquer the World With One Hand...And an Attitude* on his weekly journal, an exercise he started a few months after his stroke as part of his speech therapy.

Since publishing the first edition of this book in 1999, Paul wrote the inspirational book, also in its second edition, *You Can Do It, 105 Thoughts, Feelings and Solutions to Inspire You* (also available in audio format), and *How to Conquer Hobbies with One Hand, 50 Tips and Tools to Make Things*, also published by Positive Power Publishing. Paul is working on other books providing helpful hints at home, work and play—practical and inspirational publications on how to conquer disabilities and enjoy life. And, he plans to continue to make speeches and presentations, a remarkable achievement given his continuing struggle with severe aphasia.

Stephanie Mensh, Paul's wife and co-author, has worked as a professional advocate, policy analyst, writer, editor and manager in the healthcare field for over 20 years.

She currently serves as an Associate Vice President, Payment and Policy, for the Advanced Medical Technology Association. Previously, she served as the managing editor of Dr. Julian Whitaker's *Health & Healing*, of one of the largest circulation private consumer health newsletters.

Stephanie serves on the boards of various organizations advocating for disabled people. She is a native of the Washington, D.C. area, where she earned a B.A. in English and Politics from the American University, and a masters degree from George Mason University. Stephanie plans to write about her experiences as the spouse of a stroke survivor, and continue to join Paul in making speeches and presentations.

Positive Power Publishing

Positive Power Publishing is dedicated to inspiring people with disabilities to live a full life and to show the world that having a disability doesn't mean giving up.

Paul Berger's compelling story is an example of the can-do attitude and abilities that many disabled people offer.

Write to us, call, or visit our website for more information on ordering Paul's books, and to invite Paul and Stephanie to make an inspirational, motivational, or how-to-do-it speech to your group.

Visit our website to view TV news clips, photos from Paul's many public presentations, the NCCD award ceremony at the Kennedy Center, comments from readers, and more...

Positive Power Publishing
P.O. Box 2644
Merrifield, Virginia 22116 U.S.A.
Phone and fax: 703-241-2375
Email: info@StrokeSurvivor.com
Visit our website at: www.StrokeSurvivor.com

Read Paul Berger's Inspirational Book
You Can Do It!
105 Thoughts, Feelings &
Solutions To Inspire You

"You have inspired many people by handling your adversity in the most positive way."

—Bob Williams, stroke survivor

"This captivating book will open the inner world of the survivor of stroke or brain injury to families and professionals. It is sure to inspire hope and courage."

—Debi Gale, MS, CCC-SLP, speech pathologist

Table of Contents:
- 3 Things that Give Me Motivation
- Thoughts About My Stroke
- How It Feels to be Disabled
- My Solutions and Tips
- Tips on Finding a Job
- How I Learn to Give a Speech
- How I Conquered My Stroke

Solutions...
63. "I can't button my sleeve on my good left arm, so I use collar extenders on the cuff."

Thoughts...
11. My right arm and hand are useless—like a permanent broken arm.

Feelings...
14. "I'm slow at everything."

Tips on Finding a Job...
79. "Explore new and different types of work you can do part time, full time, or volunteer."

Do you have trouble reading?

Don't have time to read?

Now you can listen to

You Can Do It!
105, Thoughts, Feelings & Solutions to Inspire You

Available on cassette tape and audio CD

Recorded book read by
Paul's fellow Toastmaster, Nick Dunbar

"Paul's book speaks to and for those of us who have survived a traumatic brain injury. Each of the sentences reveals a hard-learned truth. Too often, we 'survivors' are forgotten or ignored...This book will be a major step in giving us a voice."
—John M. Heidemann, Jr., stroke survivor

To order your copies of the book, tape or CD, contact Positive Power Publishing, P.O. Box 2644, Merrifield, VA 22116, phone/fax: 703-241-2375, email: info@StrokeSurvivor.com, website order form: www.StrokeSurvivor.com. Visa and Master Card accepted.

Book: 32 pages • ISBN 0-9668378-2-7
Recording, 47 minutes
Cassette tape • ISBN 0-9668378-4-3
Audio CD • ISBN 0-9668378-5-1

How to Conquer Hobbies With One Hand
Stroke Survivor Paul E. Berger's
50 Tips and Tools to Make Things

"This little book is full of great ideas and product sources for the one-handed hobby enthusiast."
—Kathryn Levit, OTR

"I was impressed by the details...Very easy to read and very well organized."
—Gary Gondos, stroke survivor

"Thank you for your book and inspiration. Model railroading will be even more fun now!"
—Don Fucci, modeler

Table of Contents:
- 10 Reasons to Have a Hobby
- 5 Ways to Pick a Hobby
- A 2-Minute Tour of My Hobby
- 5 Essentials for Your Work Area
- 20 Tools for One-Handed Hobbyists
- Shopping List
- Resources
- 16 photos of tools

Special! 10 Bonus Tips

To order your copies of the book, contact Positive Power Publishing, P.O. Box 2644, Merrifield, VA 22116, phone/fax: 703-241-2375, email: info@StrokeSurvivor.com, website order form: www.StrokeSurvivor.com. Visa and Master Card accepted.

32 pages • ISBN 0-9668378-3-5